D1459340

Jenson Button

Alex **Zanardi**
my story

ISBN **1 84425 108 X**
£18.99

David **Coulthard**

ISBN **1 84425 035 0**
£15.99

Juan Pablo **Montoya**

Christopher Hilton

ISBN **1 85960 998 8**
£15.99

The Formula 1
YOUNG GUNS

Nick Garton

ISBN **1 84425 046 6**
£14.99

The science of
Formula 1
Design

David Tremayne

ISBN **1 85960 999 6**
£19.99

MICHAEL SCHUMACHER
THE GREATEST OF ALL

ISBN **1 84425 044 X**
£19.99

Jenson
Button

The unauthorised biography

Alan Henry

Haynes Publishing

**MORAY COUNCIL
LIBRARIES &
INFO.SERVICES**

20 13 96 90	
Askews	
796.72092	

© Alan Henry, 2004

All rights reserved. No part of this publication may be reproduced, stored in a retrieval system or transmitted, in any form or by any means, electronic, mechanical, photocopying, recording or otherwise, without prior permission in writing from the publisher.

First published in October 2004

A catalogue record for this book is available from the British Library

ISBN 1 84425 125 X

Library of Congress catalog card no 2004112993

Haynes North America Inc.,
861 Lawrence Drive, Newbury Park,
California 91320, USA.

Published by Haynes Publishing,
Sparkford, Yeovil, Somerset BA22 7JJ, UK.
Tel: 01963 442030 Fax: 01963 440001
Int. tel: +44 1963 442030 Int. fax: +44 1963 440001
E-mail: sales@haynes.co.uk
Website: www.haynes.co.uk

Page layout by Chris Fayers
Printed and bound in Britain by
J. H. Haynes & Co. Ltd, Sparkford

Contents

introduction
and acknowledgements

This is an informal study of Jenson Button's racing career to date. In 2004 he has emerged as a formidable contender in the Formula 1 Drivers' Championship. Nigel Mansell and Damon Hill both won World Championships against the expectations of many in the Formula 1 pit lane. At the time of writing, it looked highly likely that he would achieve his first race victory in the 2004 season. Yet, as Damon Hill shrewdly noted, you come to appreciate that there are no certainties whatsoever in Formula 1.

Button possesses the speed, talent and maturity to help drive the BAR-Honda team on to greater things, even if perhaps in 2004 the team's ambitions ran ahead of their technical capability on the circuit. Sadly, what promised to be a great partnership ran into stormy water during the summer of 2004, and Jenson is intent on returning to the BMW Williams squad for 2005.

Observing Jenson's progress has been instructive. He feels he hasn't fundamentally changed during his time in Formula 1. But I am not the only one to disagree with this assertion. Later in these pages you will read Sir Jackie Stewart's assessment of Jenson's rise to maturity. The pressure to succeed forces the pace of a driver's race to maturity in the F1 business. There is no doubt in my mind that Button is a more grown-up, rounded and complete personality than he was at the start of his career with BAR at the beginning of 2003, let alone when he started his F1 career with Williams in 2000. He is also very quick indeed.

I am particularly grateful to David Richards for the time expended discussing Jenson's progress since he arrived at BAR. I particularly appreciate the fact that he invited me to his home to dine with Jenson last year when I was preparing an article for *F1 Racing* magazine.

Although this is by no means an official biography, Jenson has always been courteous and uncomplicated when it came to answering questions posed during the general course of my day job covering the Formula 1 World Championship. He is very much his own man.

I would also like to thank Sir Jackie Stewart, Damon Hill, David and Steve Robertson, Flavio Briatore, Sir Frank Williams, Patrick Head, Warren Hughes, John Button, David Tremayne, John Fitzpatrick and Anthony Davidson for the many informal chats on the subject of Jenson's progress during his career. I am particularly grateful to John McIlroy, editor of *Autosport* and Matt Bishop, editor-in-chief of *F1 Racing*, for permission to quote from their magazines.

The admirably efficient BAR-Honda F1 press service provided by Tracy Novak, Jane Chapman, Charlie Reid and Emma Bearpark has assisted with data and statistics. My friends at LAT Photographic, Peter Higham, Kathy Ager, Tim Wright and Steven Tee have again toiled well beyond the call of duty to research and select most of the splendid photographs that illustrate these pages. Thank you all.

Alan Henry
Tillingham, Essex
July 2004

The moment he'd been waiting for. Climbing from his BAR-Honda cockpit after finishing third in the 2004 Malaysian Grand Prix, his first podium finish. (LAT)

the baby-faced kartist

There is a definite sense of pride and protection among the residents of Frome, in Somerset, towards the privacy of their most recent celebrity inhabitant. When some of Jenson Button's friends began to suspect that a national newspaper might be snooping around, trying to tempt them into dishing the dirt on the now-famous Formula 1 driver, there was an almost public plea for everybody to protect their man from what they clearly regarded as an unwarranted intrusion.

Pupils at Selwood Middle School had been approached discreetly, as were two members of Jenson's year group at Frome Community College. It sounds as though they were given short shrift. 'I know that the whole of Frome is so pleased and proud of Jenson Button and I think it is awful that no famous person's privacy is their own,' one anonymous pal told the *Somerset Standard*. 'I hope that Jenson's fellow students do not take this reporter's money and give Jenson a little respect. It's the least he deserves as he's made us all proud and put Frome on the map.'

Jenson is remembered as a polite kid, pleasant and always smiling. And one who spent a lot of time karting. One of his teachers remembers him bringing his kart into school one morning as the centrepiece for the assembly. All the locals also knew him from the familiar Transit van in which he and his father used to transport the kart to his various race meetings.

Jenson Button was born in Frome on January 19, 1980. He grew up with his three older sisters, Natasha, Samantha and Tanya. Shortly before his eighth birthday his parents separated. Afterwards his father John bought a kart from his old friend Keith Ripp, a former rallycross ace who'd built up a successful car performance accessory business. Not really knowing what the hell to do with it, John presented it to his son as a Christmas present. They took it for a preliminary test run on a disused airfield at Bridgwater. But Jenson soon tired of that and they decided to enter Jenson in his debut race at the Clay Pigeon track in Dorset, about an hour's drive from their Somerset home.

He won, first time out. At that time Jenson really thought it was just a bit of luck. But in reality, long before he even registered on the car racing fraternity's long-range radar screens, it would be his first step down a long road that would turn him into a seasoned and streetwise professional racer.

'It rained more or less all day,' John Button says. 'When he won, I did the unforgiveable thing of running out onto the track and jumping up and down. I soon learned.'

Before long Jenson was making rapid progress through the ranks of championship karting, although resources were sometimes stretched. Most weekends they would set off for a meeting, and, as Button senior told Richard Williams of *The Guardian*, their return from one race in Scotland was only made possible when he borrowed enough money to fill the tank of his van for the journey home.

Jenson climbed up through the ranks with the support of both parents, but in particular his father, who bankrolled his efforts and prepared his karts.

The smile's very familiar, even though he's still barely into his teens. (LAT)

Although his parents had decided to go their separate ways, both they and Jenson's sisters always remained incredibly supportive of his efforts to make the motor racing big time.

One of the fascinations with motor racing is the way in which competing members of various families cross one another's path from time to time. The tapestry of interrelated careers can become complex, almost interdependent. It often brings a touch of reassuring family warmth to what is fundamentally a ruthless, unforgiving and hard-edged business. 'Every karting father believes their son is something special, and I was trying to be realistic,' says John Button. 'I had no intention of racing him at all. Then someone suggested it. So I asked him if he wanted to do it; he said yes, and that was that.'

Jenson has a fine competition pedigree behind him. His father John competed against Alexander Wurz's father on the European rallycross scene back in the late 1970s. Wurz would later race against Jenson's Williams from the cockpit of a Renault R200 F1 contender. 'My father did the British and European [rallycross] championships,' explains Jenson, 'and he did quite well considering that he was not in one of the works teams. He came second in the 1978 British Championship and third in the European series in 1979, the year before I was born.' When Jenson was eight, Button senior was offered a drive in a Metro 6R4. He declined the offer because he wanted to concentrate on starting his son's kart racing career. He was very committed and supportive, and remains so to this day.

In 1991, Jenson moved up into the Cadet class. The category can only be described as a kart racing phenomenon. With some of the competitors barely within sight of their tenth birthday, the sight of a swarming pack of these pre-teenage hornets droning round in huge nose-to-tail bunches is as electrifying and intensely competitive as any F3 or Formula Ford competition.

Jenson took to it like a duck to water. In 1991, he won all 34 races in which he competed to win the British Cadet Championship. He also won the British Open title, and repeated that achievement in 1992 and 1993. In 1992 he also won the British Junior Championship.

'You don't get bored with winning,' said Jenson years later as he reflected on his kart racing days. 'Coming second and third is boring, but not winning.' Yet sustaining one's competitive edge in any category of motorsport can be a difficult balancing act. You are under the spotlight to perform all the time and the intensity of that pressure can lead you to push just a bit too hard, and go over the edge.

It happened to Button in 1994 when he was leading the British Junior series. He destroyed his chances with a series of uncharacteristic accidents. On reflection, he acknowledges that he 'lost his head a bit'. That same year he raced in the World Championship event for the famous Italian Birel factory team, kart makers of

Learning his craft, Jenson (189) pilots his Tecno kart during the CIK-FIA World Championship Karting race at Valence, France in September 1995. Jenson went on to finish second in this race. (Sutton Images)

distinction since the 1960s. Then, in 1995, with his parents' blessing, it was decided that Jenson would take the plunge and contest the Italian national championship as a professional.

'A lot of the big names in karting are from Italy,' he says, 'the teams, the chassis manufacturers and. the engine specialists. So I went there to get to know everybody.' Jenson's schooling became something of a problem, but the 14-year-old jetsetter managed to sustain some semblance of academic progress, aided by additional tuition at evening classes. Under the

circumstances he was pretty successful, although he rather shamefacedly confessed that his Italian never progressed much beyond the language of the kart track pit lane.

Between winning the British Cadet Championship at 11 years old and the European Championship at 17, Jenson acquired a reasonably rounded education. Early in his racing career, his junior and middle-school classmates knew nothing of his sporting prowess. But by the time he arrived at Frome College to study for his GCSEs, it was impossible to disguise the reason for his

One for the
trophy cupboard.
Jenson displays
the spoils of
victory at the
1995 *Autosport*
Show. (LAT)

Celebrating
victory in the
1997 European
Kart
Championship
(Sutton Images)

top drive and he was signed by the Team GKS using works Tecno-Rotax karts. He finished fifth in the European Formula A Championship and the team decided to put him into Formula Super A for 1997. The rest is history. 'It was the Formula 1 of karting,' Jenson explains, 'and it is very professional compared to Formula Ford, for example. People pay the same kind of money to race in Formula Ford.'

In addition to the European title Button also won the Ayrton Senna Memorial Cup at Suzuka. 'It is not automatically the winner of the race who wins the cup,' he says. 'They pick the driver that reminds them most of Senna and I was lucky enough to win it.'

What he modestly keeps to himself is that in the pre-final race he started 18th and finished in the wheel tracks of the winner. He also makes no mention of the fact that he was fighting for the lead in the final when the chain on his kart snapped. The President of the International Karting Federation Ernest Buser was prompted to remark, 'Jenson reminds me of Senna'.

The problem with Jenson winning the European Championship at his first attempt was that there was precious little point in his staying in Formula Super A, so Button made the jump to car racing. By the end of 1997 he could look back with a huge sense of satisfaction. His achievements over the previous nine years had been remarkable. A generation earlier, any bright young talent seeking to cut a path through to a career as a professional racing driver would have had their hands full making any impact at all.

They might have done some kart racing, sure enough, but back then the junior category in motorsport was more self-contained. By the 1990s it had matured into an accepted feeder category for the junior ranks of single-seater car racing. In the 1970s, one's head would be turned by news that a 17-year-old was producing

absences. Nevertheless, he is recalled with affection for refusing to exploit his achievements. 'He kept the two worlds firmly separate,' Dave Kitchener, his old form tutor, told *The Guardian*. 'He was a regular member of the community, and that was why he was so well liked. If you asked him about what he was up to, he'd tell you. But there was no boasting or bragging.'

Jenson was also suitably downbeat about his achievements. 'At school I did well in French but I couldn't speak a word of it, so I really don't know how I did that and in Italy I picked up a bit of the language,' he says. 'I could speak to the mechanics about the chassis but the biggest problem was that they all spoke English so it made it very difficult to learn Italian.' Nevertheless, Button astounded the karting fraternity by winning the Italian title first time out, scoring twice as many points as the runner-up. In the World Championship he led most of the way but his tyres went off and he finished second.

It was inevitable that for 1996 Button would get a

consistently impressive results in Formula Ford. But by the time it was Jenson's turn to climb the ladder, kart racing was providing an environment in which a youngster could amass almost ten years of racing experience even before he'd passed his test to gain a driving licence for the road.

Button's achievement of taking the European Formula Super A series in his maiden was a first; he was also the first British driver to take the crown as well as being the youngest ever to do it. In achieving this, the wide-eyed young Brit elevated himself onto a distinguished list of previous winners, which included Jarno Trulli, with whom he would later be partnered in the Renault F1 squad, and CART champion Alex Zanardi, ironically the man Button would take over from in the Williams Formula 1 team for the 2000 season.

Winning the European kart title involved competing in eight events. You had to demonstrate sufficient speed and race craft to fend off the opposition and the consistency and judgement to ensure that you're still running at the end. It may seem like stating the obvious, but striking such a successful balance has often proved beyond many who one might imagine would scale the sport's upper reaches if their merit was assessed on pure speed alone.

Karting, of course, is a split-second environment in which identifying the true future stars from those who are simply very good is an imprecise science. Some would say that luck and being in the right machinery at the right moment is the real key, but consistency is the crucial element that marks the genuine star apart.

During his climb to karting prominence, Jenson would also make the acquaintance of several other bright-eyed young chargers, all of whom wanted to make the big time and even dreamed that one day they might graduate to Formula 1. Most prominent among this elite group of Button's friends were Anthony Davidson, by 2004 running alongside Jenson in the BAR-Honda F1 team as third driver, and Dan Wheldon who is now one of the front runners in the Indy Racing League. 'We always knew that one of us would make it big,' says Davidson. 'We just didn't know which one of us, but we thought it was just possible that we could all be there.'

'We just had a feeling about making it a long time ago,' adds Wheldon. 'We knew we had talent and the things it would take. We were only eight, nine years old at the time but somehow we felt we knew. It's funny, but circumstances mean that we don't see each other that often anymore, but when we do it's like we've been together for ever. It takes us about five minutes to catch up.'

'We were always beating each other and it was good fun,' recalls Jenson. 'We were friends, too, which made it nice. We were just kids, but we were learning to be competitive.'

Now came a turning point. Jenson had reached the pinnacle of karting and would now have to move forward into cars. But to do that meant raising funds that were certainly beyond the means of John Button. Graduating into Formula Ford 1600 for 1998 was probably going to cost around £90,000. So unless John and Jenson could find some hard backing, and soon, the boy's racing career and lifelong hopes faced the very real danger of stalling in the pit lane.

Following in the footsteps of a legend. Jenson sports a 'Senninha' t-shirt. Senninha is a cartoon character inspired by the great Ayrton Senna. (LAT)

into
formula
ford

Jenson's graduation from karting into the British FF1600 Championship took place in 1998. In fact he considered making the jump straight into F3, but resisted the temptation after discussions with David Robertson and Harald Huysman, both of whom were to be key players in shaping and organising his early career. Robertson, in particular, was a fan of Button's talent from an early age. He and his son Steve later discovered Kimi Raikkonen, of course, and subsequently lost their role as Button's managers to John Byfield of Essentially Sport.

In May 1998, in a restaurant in the centre of Barcelona, Huysman, a former Formula 3 driver, and a British businessman by the name of David Robertson introduced a small group of journalists to a slim, well groomed young man. He made an impact, but not that big an impact. He had a pleasant character, and looked you straight in the eye. But did he have what it takes to mark him out from the rest of the ambitious young Brit pack, all aiming for the top, all determined to break into Formula 1?

That was the first meeting with Jenson Button for a number of British Formula 1 press corps. The only one

Growing up. Early in his Formula Ford career at Thruxton, April 1998, barely 18 years old and just out of karts. (LAT)

Influential people. Jenson meets Frank Williams during his visit to the 1998 Spanish Grand Prix at Barcelona, which Keith Sutton arranged with Bernie Ecclestone. (LAT)

who had really been keeping a close eye on him had been David Tremayne of *The Independent*, who had been alerted to his potential on the strength of his kart racing achievements. Tremayne would be as loyal an advocate of Button's cause over the next few years as the rest of us would be sceptics. He kept the faith as Jenson duly ploughed his way through Formula Ford, Formula 3 and right up to that moment when a driver fumbles his big chance or makes the most of the Formula 1 test driving opportunity when it finally arrives.

But in a sense Jenson stuck his foot in the Formula 1 door when he made that timely visit to the Circuit de Catalunya. As my colleague Richard Williams of *The Guardian* rightly noted, this track laid out amid the dreary industrial zones that separate Barcelona from the mountains hardly throbs with the history and romance of Grand Prix history in the same way as such long-forgotten circuits as Sitges or Pedralbes. Yet this was the weekend on which the bright-eyed teenager first swiped his computerised visitor's pass through the security barrier to gain access to that holiest of holies, the Grand Prix paddock. He was taken around by his managers and duly photographed with Bernie Ecclestone, Frank Williams and Ron Dennis, key people he would meet again as his career unfolded.

At the age of 18 Button had made the transition from karts to cars and found himself a shrewd management team in Huysman and the Robertsons. They invested heavily in Button's career in return for a 35 per cent share of his future income, and enlisted the help of Keith Sutton, a motor racing photographer who had helped publicise Ayrton Senna's early career. In return for putting his agency's logo on Button's virgin-white car, Sutton used his contacts to spread the word about the young driver's talent.

It was Sutton who persuaded Bernie Ecclestone to grant Button a paddock pass for the Spanish Grand Prix in 1998. He also put together a sponsorship proposal when Button moved up to Formula 3 the following year, and helped attract Frank Williams's attention 18 months later when Alain Prost offered Button a test in his Formula 1 car, again at Barcelona.

David Robertson was rich, and a streetwise wheeler dealer with a roguish charm. His deep knowledge of motorsport was buttressed by the achievements of his son Steve. The younger Robertson had raced competitively in the British Formula 3 Championship, handled a works Ford Mondeo in the British Touring Car Championship and also competed in the US with distinction, winning the 1994 Indy Lights Championship, the feeder series for Champcar. Huysman had also been an accomplished Formula 3 contender, so between them, the three men could deploy an almost unique combination of financial resource, racing savvy and business judgement.

David Robertson was keen to identify and bring on a new British talent. He fancied the challenge, the gamble, if you like, of investing in a new rising star, of having his judgement proved correct. It would also prove to be an astute investment. Bankrolling a bright young star's entry to single-seater racing would require a significant cash investment. But with a multi-year management contract in place guaranteeing a healthy slice of that driver's income, maybe as much as 40 per cent for up to five years, if he made it into Formula 1, it would be jackpot time for Robertson and Huysman. But the real question was just who to back?

'Jenson was first brought to my attention by Harald,' he says. 'He had heard about him from some guy he knew in Belgium who was involved in karting and he

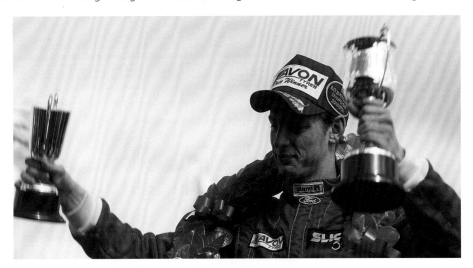

Celebrating his second Formula Ford victory, on the rostrum at Donington Park on 4 May 1998. (LAT)

In the cockpit of the Mygale, almost ready for action, Brands Hatch in May 1998. Jenson's sunny disposition was rarely clouded by short-term racing misfortunes, even at this early stage in his career. (LAT)

Looking pensive with father John (left) in the paddock at the Croft circuit, near Darlington, June 1998. (LAT)

Button in smooth action at Croft. He finished third in the race, behind Dan Wheldon and Marcos Ambrose in the works Van Diemens. (LAT)

reckoned Jenson was the best talent he'd seen since Ayrton Senna. Meanwhile I also spoke to Terry Fullerton, who was one of the handful of kart racers that Senna really rated. So all the evidence came together pointing to the fact that Jenson was the guy we should look after. By this stage Jenson had already been promised some funds from another source to go car racing, but it all fell through leaving him in limbo. So I put a call in to John Button, we had a brief chat and arranged to meet up. So that was basically when we put pen to paper and the moment was ripe for him to make the step forward into cars, which he did in 1998.

'Harald originally hadn't any intention of investing in Jenson,' adds Robertson, 'but he eventually came in, paid half and we committed to financing him through. My son Steve, who, of course, knows a lot about motor racing, told me I was mad, that the chances of getting Jenson through were pretty slim. I told him, well, I was going to take that chance, because if you think he's good enough – which Steve also clearly did – then I thought that we were good enough to get him there, because we knew motorsport pretty well.'

Yet Jenson's commitment to karting was very deep-rooted. Although he was determined to climb the single-seater ladder, he knew he would miss the split-second competition and close camaraderie of a world that had absorbed his attention for virtually ten years, almost as long as he could remember.

'I didn't miss karting until this year when I saw pictures and read the results of the last few races,' he reflected as he looked back on his Formula Ford career. 'I have been in karting for nine years and I miss it. I would like to do some more races but obviously it is not easy with what I am doing now. Formula Ford is a lot slower than we were in karts, but it is a good formula to start out in because you learn a lot of race craft and engineering. Single seaters and karts are different.'

Before racing in Formula Ford Button received his first taste of Formula 3 with a test of a 1997 Dallara, run by Carlin Motorsport, at the Pembrey circuit, near Llanelli, in south Wales. 'It went very well,' Jenson recalled to Joe Saward of the influential *grandprix.com* website. 'Warren Hughes was testing at the same time with a Renault engine and a 1998-spec car and I did a time which was three tenths slower with an engine that was at the end of its mileage. I was very pleased. Actually I wasn't. At the time I was a bit disappointed because I don't like people going faster than me even if it was my first test in an F3 car. I was a bit down. Formula 3 seems to be a bit more interesting than Formula Ford although at that stage I hadn't actually raced an F3 car. It was easier to drive because there was a lot more grip and downforce and that is why the times are a lot closer. In Formula Ford you have no wings and so you slide.'

For his part, Hughes was impressed. 'To be in the ballpark immediately was extremely impressive on Jenson's part, irrespective of the comparative speed between us. He was extremely smooth and that would later come into much sharper perspective when Jenson did a full season of F3 in 1999. More than in most categories of racing, in F3 smoothness is the key. You have to apply controlled aggression, aggression to the point where you are not over-driving the car and losing speed. I think Jenson had that point well sussed from an early age.'

Yet there was a huge risk involved in making the transition straight from karting to F3, even for a youngster of Button's undoubted potential. Learning how to drive a single seater effectively would be a big

enough challenge in itself without grappling to make sense of slicks and aerodynamic downforce at the same time. Even the great Ayrton Senna progressed gradually through Formula Ford, then FF2000 and into Formula 3 over the course of three seasons. That said, Steve Robertson, who made the trip to that Pembrey test, reported back that he was extremely impressed with Jenson's composure. His father David was keen that Jenson should make the big jump, but the teenager was reluctant to do so.

Thus with the same decisive confidence he would display two years later in assuring his concerned father John that he was actually ready for the graduation into Formula 1, Jenson Button now took what might have been seen as a more conservative decision. Every young driver is aware that second chances in professional motor racing are generally few and far between. At barely 18 years old Jenson didn't need to be taking too many risks with his career. As Nelson Angelo Piquet, son of Brazil's triple World Champion Nelson, demonstrated in 2003–4, trying to run before you can walk as an apparent teenage Formula 3 prodigy can wreak serious damage to your career prospects. Young Piquet was

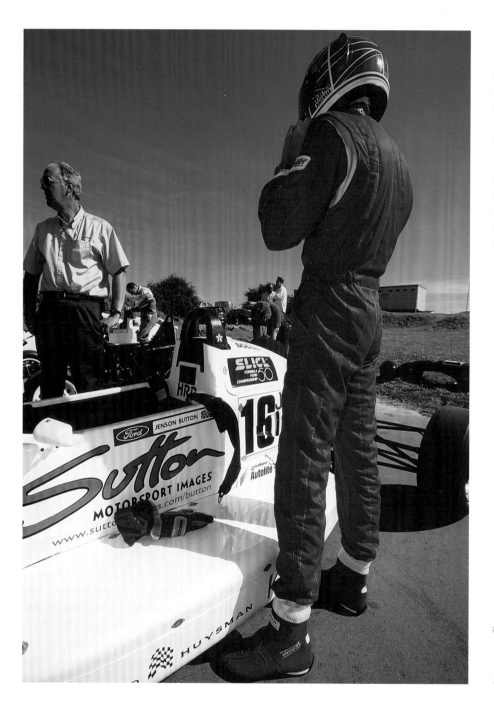

Ready for action at Snetterton, in July '98. Keith Sutton, shrewd as always, has his company's identification on the side of the young racer's car, backing him as he did Senna two decades before. (LAT)

Showing a clean pair of heels to the rest of the TOCA Slick 50 Formula Ford pack on the opening lap at Snetterton. Jenson would eventually finish second behind Dan Wheldon. (LAT)

August 1998, just four months into his Formula Ford racing career, and even at this early stage Jenson is visually more seasoned and mature. (LAT)

barely 18 when he had his first F1 test in a Williams-BMW and, by all accounts, it was a little premature even allowing for his obvious talent. The same could well have happened to Jenson if he'd missed out Formula Ford and gone directly into F3.

In the event, Button persuaded David Robertson that he should go with Jim Warren's Haywood Racing operation where he would be partnered by Derek Hayes and pitched up against some of his old karting rivals, most notably Dan Wheldon who was regarded as one of the pre-season favourites. Despite predictions that he was unlikely to be competitive in his first season of Formula Ford, and that Haywood's Mygale chassis would not be a match for the latest Van Diemen, Jenson made the transition with a seamless efficiency that may have surprised some observers but not those who'd been monitoring his progress in the world of karting.

Jenson finished third in his first race and quickly got into the swing of things, mastering the subtle nuances of racing and qualifying technique with an assured confidence, even though the gamesmanship displayed by his rivals sometimes caught him by surprise. On his first outing at Silverstone, for example, he had problems in qualifying. 'I had been quite fast in testing, so when I went out to qualify the first few laps were a nightmare because I had about six people behind me trying to see what I was doing and every lap I had people slowing down so they could get behind me and that was slowing me down,' he says. 'I came in after ten minutes and told the crew that there was no point in going out because I just could not get a good lap and that it was better to wait until the very end. I waited for the last four minutes and then went for it and I put the car on pole, a tenth off the lap record.'

Nose to nose with team-mate and title rival Derek Hayes at Brands Hatch in September 1998. Jenson finished second in the first heat to win the title, celebrating with a win in the second heat. (LAT)

Under increasing pressure as the season wore on, Jenson survived some other instructive experiences including being excluded from a meeting at Brands Hatch after he'd overtaken Dan Wheldon under a yellow caution flag as they battled for the lead. Button explained that Wheldon's car had effectively masked his view of the flag and that he was unaware of his accidental transgression. He felt it was a bit much excluding him from the entire meeting, but he filed the experience away in his personal memory bank and learned from the experience.

Jenson's successful efforts in winning the TOCA Slick 50 Formula Ford 1600 Championship crown put him in pole position for the BRDC McLaren *Autosport* young driver of the year award. He also had a victory in the Brands Hatch Formula Ford Festival and runner-up status in the Euroseries to embellish his personal CV. With a cheque for £50,000, a test drive in a McLaren-

Leading Haywood
Racing team-mate
Derek Hayes in
his Formula Ford
Mygale at Brands
Hatch in August
1998. (LAT)

The candidates
for the 1998
BRDC McLaren
Autosport
award pose in
their competition

overalls. The
winner is beaming
confidently,
second from
the left.
(LAT)

Mercedes F1 car and sheafs of free publicity, this is the most coveted award a young driver can receive. By any standards, it is a sensational prize and involves a programme of detailed analysis, observation and assessment at a carefully structured test session held at Silverstone, the home of the BRDC.

In Jenson's year this involved first driving a Lotus Elise from the Silverstone Racing School. Then an F3 Dallara-Mugen provided by Alan Docking Racing, which is

based at the track, and finally a Nissan Primera touring car. Then the candidates were subjected to a videoed interview to test their social and communication skills. Then the judges decided that they wanted all the candidates to return again on another day and repeat the whole procedure again. Jenson would admit that he found the off-track interviews stressful, but intriguing. But he needn't have worried.

There was another highly respected racing

All spiffed up in five-star luxury. Jenson dressed in racing kit at London's Grosvenor House Hotel in December 1998 prior to changing into his dinner jacket to receive the prize that would transform his life. (LAT)

Amazing moment. With BBC's Steve Rider at the presentation of the 1998 BRDC McLaren *Autosport* Young Driver of the Year. Jenson pocketed a cheque for £50,000, which gave him a flying start to his F3 career. (LAT)

personality who had no doubts about Button's potential from an early stage. This was John Fitzpatrick, BRDC club secretary and a member of the judging panel for the BRDC McLaren *Autosport* awards for many years in the 1990s. Speaking to the author shortly after Jenson bagged his first F1 pole position at Imola in 2004, he made it clear that the young British driver's progress had come as no surprise to him.

'I remember when he walked in the door of the BRDC suite on the first morning of the testing,' said Fitzpatrick. 'He looked like a winner, the way he carried himself and talked. Strange how you can tell before they even get into the car. As secretary of the BRDC,

I was the organiser and chairman of the judges for the award from 1993 until 1999 when I left BRDC. I was one of five judges.

'It was a rule that the boys had to come alone, without parents or friends. The weather over the two days was atrocious and we had to schedule an extra day. In those circumstances you would have expected them to be a little nervous but Jenson was supremely confident and outstanding in the wet.

'In fact Nick Faldo, in one of his articles in *The Times* recently also quoted what I said about being able to assess a young driver before he even sat in the car, because he too, in his support of young golfers, said he

Getting his reward. Almost a year after winning the BRDC McLaren *Autosport* award, Jenson tries his hand in a McLaren-Mercedes F1 car on a damp track at Silverstone. It is November 1999 and by now he has a year's experience in F3 under his belt. (LAT)

was able to judge a young golfer by the way he walked on the tee and took his club out of the bag.' And Jenson duly won the day, following in the wheel tracks of such celebrated names as David Coulthard and Dario Franchitti.

With his cheque for £50,000 safely tucked away as a deposit in preparation for the cost of a Formula 3 season, Button could really enjoy every second of his outing in a McLaren-Mercedes F1 car, a test that took place in the rather depressing surroundings of a wet Silverstone one dank morning in November 1999. The track was wet enough for rain tyres to be deployed, even though the track was starting to dry out by the time Jenson got into the swing of things. He completed his first ten-lap run and came into the pits to think things over. Then did just eight laps of his allotted second ten-lap stint before coming in and telling the team that, as the tyre treads were starting to chunk on the drying tarmac, he'd better call it a day there and then.

Dave Ryan, the McLaren team manager and a veteran of 24 years with the company, was impressed. Not so much with the speed and assurance which Jenson had demonstrated behind the wheel, but more by his assurance and general all-round polish. 'The guy handled himself incredibly well,' Ryan told David Tremayne, 'just

the way he approached it, the way he drove the car. He used the radio and it just seemed natural to him. He told us what he was doing all the time.'

Impressing an experienced, no-nonsense professional like Ryan was something of which Button could be rightly proud. McLaren is a tough operation that has been there, done it all, seen it all before. In four decades it has seen some of the greatest contemporary F1 drivers pass through its system. That Jenson struck the right note was as impressive as it was promising.

At around this stage in his career, Button also received an approach to meet the McLaren chairman Ron Dennis. After some polite small talk, Dennis asked Robertson and Huysman if they would mind waiting downstairs in the reception area. According to Button, once they had absented themselves, Dennis suggested that Jenson ditch them as his management team and come in with McLaren instead. With commendable loyalty, Button declined the offer. The irony here, of course, is that Dennis would later find himself negotiating with David Robertson in order to secure the services of Kimi Raikkonen in 2002. By that time Jenson would have severed the business partnership with his original managers and thrown in his lot with John Byfield's Essentially Sport operation.

A step up the ladder. Jenson moved into Formula 3 with the Promatecme team for 1999. (LAT)

formula 3 break

Jenson moved into Formula 3 in 1999 with the Silverstone-based Promatecme team, driving a Renault-engined Dallara, which wasn't the most competitive machine in the field. He finished third in the championship which was won by fellow Brit Marc Hynes. Yet it is testimony to the unpredictability of the motor racing business that Hynes's career effectively stalled thereafter and Button's accelerated towards the stars. What made the difference? Astute management, good contacts, or just the fact that Button was better?

Winning the British F3 Championship has historically opened doors to a Formula 1 test drive, or in recent years it at least ensured that the driver concerned was in the pound seats when it came to securing a Formula 3000 test drive. Yet the fact of the matter is that money talks. Button would benefit in this respect not simply from the fact that the Robertsons had backed his early progress with hard cash, but that they had an interest in ensuring he advanced up the ladder as quickly as was prudent in order to ensure a return on their investment.

The British F1 season basically came down to a tussle between Hynes, the 21-year-old from Gloucestershire, and Luciano Burti, the young Brazilian who would later join the Jaguar F1 team. Hynes had won the British Formula Renault title in 1997 driving for the Manor Motorsport team, then moved elsewhere for an unsuccessful maiden F3 season, before returning to the Manor operation when it took the decision to move up a gear and graduate to F3 in 1999. Armed with the familiar Dallara chassis powered by a Mugen-Honda engine, Hynes got off to a flying start by winning the first two races. Later he added another three victories, including the British Grand Prix supporting race and the prestigious Marlboro Masters event at Zandvoort, the seaside circuit near Haarlem that used to host the Dutch Grand Prix.

Hynes was ranged against Burti who was driving for the blue riband Paul Stewart Racing operation. Burti struggled to get the best out of the Dallara F399 in the early races of the season and only really got things under control by late summer following an intensive programme of test and development work. Branded the best of the rest was Jenson, driving a Renault-engined Dallara for the Silverstone-based Promatecme team. The 19-year-old won three races and made plenty of mistakes, which reflected the fact that he was only two years out of kart racing, yet he managed to mark himself out as probably the best young driver on the UK Formula 3 starting grids.

It had been a long, hard winter. At the end of his Formula Ford season, there had been offers from at least two Formula 3 teams for him to race in the important Macau Grand Prix meeting in the Far East. Jenson declined the offers, flattered though he was, as he appreciated that this might be a little too over-optimistic a move to make at this stage of his career. But Keith Sutton was monitoring the situation closely. For Jenson Button, the old adage that states it's not what you know but who you know was about to come true, and not for the first time in his career.

Sutton went to the final F3 meeting of the 1998 season and met up with Promatecme boss Serge Saulnier who he knew through his thriving Sutton Motorsport Images business, which was based in nearby Towcester. Keith had developed a keen feel for promising young drivers over the past couple of decades, from the time he homed in on Ayrton Senna's peerless genius when the Brazilian was racing in FF2000 back in 1982. It was getting a bit late in the day to arrange a decent F3 drive for Jenson, but Sutton knew his stuff and was an ace salesman. He spoke to Saulnier and Tim Jackson, Renault UK's PR director. Saulnier was eventually bowled over by Sutton's sales pitch and offered to give Jenson a test outing at Magny-Cours.

Tim Jackson had made the point that it was Renault's general policy to support drivers who'd graduated from their junior formulae. But, for all that, he seemed quite open-minded towards Jenson. So he went to do the test at Magny-Cours and Saulnier was immediately impressed, noting the precision and accuracy with which Jenson picked up the racing lines even though he'd never driven at Magny-Cours before. By the end of the afternoon Saulnier made a commitment. He felt that in Jenson he'd just seen something extremely

Despite its Renault engine having less power than the rival Mugen Honda units, the Promatecme Dallara carried Jenson to third place in the 1999 British F3 Championship behind Marc Hynes and Luciano Burti. [LAT]

Jenson's first F3 race, at Donington in 1999, proved his quality. He started from pole, and finished second behind eventual 1999 British F3 Champion Marc Hynes, with whom he is seen here on the rostrum. [LAT]

special, and he wasn't about to let him slip through his fingers. He wanted the 18-year-old to have the drive.

Button's pure quality went on immediate display. The opening round of the British F3 contest took place at Donington Park where Jenson displayed his in-bred car control by qualifying his Dallara-Renault on pole position in the soaking conditions. Things dried out for the race, which Hynes won by just under 4 seconds from Jenson and posted fastest lap to boot. Burti was third ahead of the promising Indian rising star Narain Karthikeyan.

Jenson could only finish sixth in round two at Silverstone, but he held everybody's attention by posting his first F3 win at Thruxton in round three, trailed home by Paul Stewart runner Andrew Kirkcaldy with Hynes in third place. Button qualified second, and then stormed away to win. Marcus Simmons wrote in *Autocourse*: 'This young man exudes star quality and, at the end of the season, was agonising over the tricky decision of whether to stay in F3 for a second season – for which he would be clear title favourite – or make an early step to Formula 3000.'

With just three of the season's 16 races completed Jenson held second place in the British F3 Championship table with 43 points, just ten adrift of Marc Hynes. Yet Jenson could take nothing for granted. A fortnight later came the Brands Hatch 'double header' event where everything seemed to go wrong. He qualified fourth and fifth, and finished eighth and seventh in races won respectively by Luciano Burti and Narain Karthikeyan. Granted, Jenson had boosted his points total to 53, but Hynes – who'd finished third and sixth in the two events – now led the championship with 73 points; Burti's successes had vaulted him into second place ahead of the Promatecme driver on 57 points.

For Button, the overwhelming problem was the Renault engine's comparative lack of power when pitched against the rival Mugen-Honda propelled machines. Part of the problem seemed to stem from the fact that the preparation of the engines had been switched from Renault Sport to the specialist preparation company Sodemo. The resultant lack of straight line speed was painfully frustrating, but it was an instructive experience for Jenson in the sense that he quickly learned to control his disappointment and be very measured in his observations about the engine's shortcomings. After all, Saulnier had given him his chance to make the move up to F3, investing a great deal of confidence in his potential and Promatecme was the factory Renault representative in the British Championship.

Burti won again at Oulton Park, leading home the fast but inconsistent Danish driver Kristian Kolby by a couple of seconds with Matt Davies and Andrew Kirkcaldy next up before Jenson took the flag in fifth place, 5 seconds behind the winner. It was a strong

Jenson's first F3 win, Thruxton, 11 April 1999. Serge Saulnier, boss of the Silverstone-based Promatecme team, had no doubts about Button's potential after testing him at Magny-Cours the previous autumn. (LAT)

Chasing Hynes for all he's worth at the British Grand Prix meeting. Jenson was only 0.4 seconds behind the March at the flag, despite having a less powerful engine. (LAT)

Into battle! Jenson's Promatecme Dallara leaves the paddock to take up position on the front row of the grid, alongside Marc Hynes's Mugen-Honda at the British Grand Prix meeting at Silverstone in July 1999. (LAT)

Jenson battles with Marc Hynes's Mugen-Honda as they enter Vale during the first lap of the British Grand Prix supporting race. (LAT)

performance at the challenging Cheshire parkland circuit, but the sense of expectancy generated by that early win obviously took some of the gloss off his achievement and the gaps separating the leading contenders in the British F3 series were obviously very close indeed.

At Croft in June Button failed to finish after the throttle stuck open; that was followed up with a sixth at Brands Hatch from third on the grid. The British Grand Prix supporting race at Silverstone was obviously a big deal for the F3 brigade, but Marc Hynes had the measure of the opposition in qualifying, storming to pole position with Jenson claiming second place on the front row of the grid. Jenson made the best start and led the opening half lap as far as Vale before Hynes nipped past, in part due to Button's unfamiliarity with the technique of running quickly from a standing start on cold tyres. He kept up the pressure and finished just 0.4

With winner Marc Hynes and third placed Luciano Burti after splitting them to take second place in the F3 race at Donington Park, 5 September 1999. (LAT)

Jenson at speed in the Dallara-Renault at the final round of the 1999 British F3 Championship at Thruxton, 17 October 1999. He qualified fourth, but had a troubled race and was eliminated in a tangle with Andrew Kirkcaldy. (All LAT)

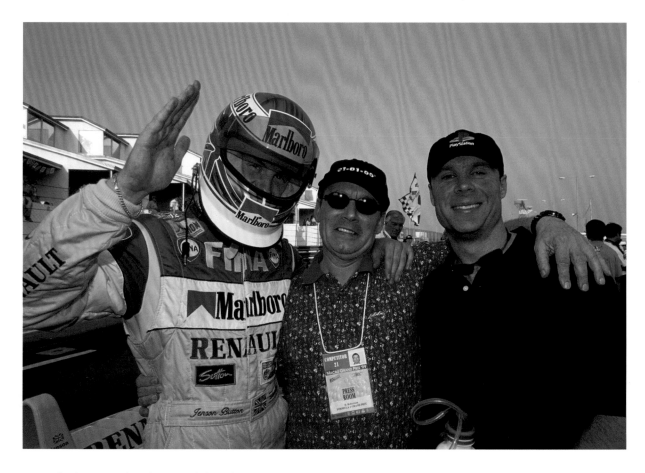

seconds down at the chequered flag, having claimed the consolation of posting the fastest race lap of 109.896mph. It was a good showing by any standards, but Jenson had now dropped to fourth place in the championship standings. Hynes now led on 124 points from Burti (121), Karthikeyan (88) and Button (83).

A fortnight after the British GP the F3 title chase moved on to Snetterton, that bleak Norfolk airfield track far removed from the glitz and glamour of Silverstone at Grand Prix time. Button qualified fourth, but got carried away with the intensity of his battle for the lead against Burti and made a rare slip, spinning to the back of the field. After a long haul back through the field he gained a distant 11th place. Admittedly this netted him two valuable points, boosting his tally to 85, but Kristian Kolby was now only six points behind him in fifth place. If Jenson was to improve his position in the championship he needed to act fast.

Before the next F3 championship 'double header,' scheduled for the Pembrey track in West Wales on 15 August, Button took a trip across to Zandvoort for the prestigious one-off Marlboro Masters F3 classic the weekend immediately prior to the Welsh fixture. Hynes won again ahead of Germany's Thomas Mutsch, Etienne dan der Line and Christjian Albers; Button came fifth. But Pembrey marked the real turnaround in Jenson's British F3 fortunes. He finished second to Kolby in the first race, then won the second from pole position, setting the fastest race laps in both events. Burti now led the championship on 157 points, just two ahead of Hynes, with Button now firmly ensconced again in third place on 122. Jenson now seemed to have regained some worthwhile momentum and he sustained that through to the Donington Park fixture on 5 September where again he finished second to Hynes and ahead of Burti, edging

Jenson with David Robertson (centre) and Harald Huysman at the Macau F3 Grand Prix in 1999. (Sutton Images)

Letting his hair down in Korea where he finished second to Darren Manning in the high-profile F3 International at the end of 1999. (LAT)

him closer to the Brazilian in the battle for second place in the championship.

There followed a three-week break in the F3 schedule after which the competitors crossed the Channel yet again, this time for a round of the British Championship on the daunting swerves of Spa-Francorchamps. Less than a year later, Jenson would qualify third on the grid for the Belgian Grand Prix in a Williams-BMW F1 car. But for the moment the challenge of the Fina F3 Masters event lay ahead around 14 gruelling laps of the spectacular 4.330-mile circuit. Superbly, Jenson qualified on pole with a lap of 114.464mph, but in the race he seemed initially to lack the sheer speed required to run with the leaders and had to settle for fourth, 6 seconds behind the victorious Burti.

Finally at Silverstone on 10 October Burti and Hynes tangled and Jenson managed to outbrake Matt Davies to take the lead and race home to post his third F3

victory of the season; he won by 6 seconds with Hynes recovering to finish third. Button was anxious to win again in the season finale at Thruxton on 17 October, but after a poor start from fourth on the grid he ran down in seventh place for the first few laps. He later tangled with Andrew Kirkcaldy, which resulted in his retirement from the race. Hynes emerged as F3 champion on 213 points ahead of Burti (209) and Jenson on 168.

After the European season ended Jenson made a trip to the Far East to contest both the Macau and Korean F3 Grands Prix. He finished second in both behind Darren Manning's Dallara-Toyota. On the face of it, Jenson's best route forward would be a second season in British F3 with championship victory firmly in his sights. But, as I said earlier, one of motorsport's most endearing qualities is its dramatic unpredictability. As Jenson would find out over the next couple of months.

The big time! Jenson strolls confidently through the paddock, a Formula 1 driver at last. (LAT)

on the
threshold
of formula 1

By the end of the 1999 season Jenson had certainly made his mark in F3. He'd finished third in the British Championship despite running with a less powerful engine than his key rivals and he had earned himself a reputation as an immaculately smooth young driver. He made few unforced errors, thought things through clearly and didn't allow himself to get flustered under pressure. Yet, for all his proven prowess, the key question of where he went next weighed heavily on the Robertsons' shoulders. They had steered and funded his career so far to great effect, but the options facing them were now less clear cut. Should they try to cut a deal to move Button into Formula 3000? Or should they go for broke and encourage him to make the jump to Formula 1?

'At the end of the day we weren't exactly inundated with offers, but during his time in Formula 3 in 1999 we put together a package which ensured that the F1 teams were at all times aware of what he was up to. He did a great job in Formula Ford, but of course didn't have the most competitive engine in Formula 3. But we were still able to establish his reputation firmly in their eyes. We were able to say "get in now, the boy's ready for F1". So he got in the Prost and showed he was a natural.

'As far as McLaren was concerned, yes there was an opportunity, but I didn't like the terms and we turned it down. Stewart was the same, basically "we want to own you", and these terms were not satisfactory either. Of course these teams were not used to people turning

them down so we weren't too popular, but I think they all appreciate now that we were probably right to turn them down. We just didn't see McLaren at that point in time, with the number of drivers they had at their disposal, as the right team . . . We believed we could get a better deal for him elsewhere.'

On the face of it, for the grand prix hopeful a move into Formula 3000 seemed to be the most logical path. This series had turned up a good number of F1 competitors over the previous decade and a half, including Jean Alesi, Olivier Panis, Nick Heidfeld and Justin Wilson. The category had certainly developed into a fertile breeding ground for new talent, but it was not without its shortcomings. Although the series featured as the main supporting event on the programme at most European grands prix, by the end of the 1990s there were lingering doubts about the strength in depth of its competition. It was also shaded by F1 in the sense that anybody wanting commercial exposure in motorsport was more likely to be attracted by the sponsorship possibilities available in the grand prix paddock rather than committing their investment to a category with a second-class image.

Button and his managers decided to take things carefully. They knew it would be wise to take a long look at Formula 3000, but they were not totally convinced. Jenson was invited down to the Jerez track in the autumn of 1999 where he tested F3000 cars fielded by two of the most experienced teams in the business, Super Nova and Fortec. He was suitably

Jenson's first serious test in a Formula 1 car came at Barcelona in the Prost AP02-Peugeot. The level of confidence and immediate assurance he displayed amazed the French team personnel. (Sutton Images)

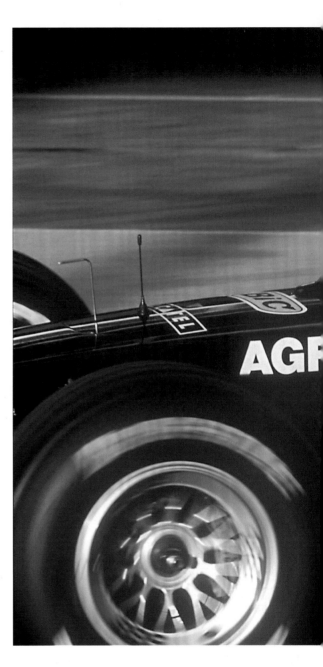

competitive and performed well, but he felt the cars were a little on the heavy side and the drop-off in performance as the tyres wore down was also a little frustrating. Jenson and the Robertsons also knew that if you didn't get into the right team at the right time, with the right budget and the best engineer, the chances of being eclipsed by ostensibly more talented drivers was a big risk indeed.

Yet another opportunity would present itself. Harald Huysman and the Robertsons were put in touch with Alain Prost who'd heard what a good job Jenson had been doing in F3. They met at Monza during the 1999 Italian Grand Prix weekend where the French team boss offered Jenson a test in one of his cars at Barcelona's Circuit de Catalunya. They moved carefully at first, grateful for the offer. But while they had total confidence in Jenson's ability to handle the situation, it was made clear to Prost that they were not prepared to sign any sort of conditional long-term option that might bind Jenson to the team beyond this one-off outing.

Many team principals would have brought negotiations to a halt there and then. Offering a test drive in exchange for first call on the services of a promising young driver was a technique well established in F1 circles and, taken at face value, it seemed extremely reasonable. With the on-track running costs of an F1 car approaching $1,500 a lap at the time Jenson was offered the Prost drive, it seemed an understandable *quid pro quo* for the team owner to take an option on the driver's services. After all, if the team was to be responsible for promoting the career of a future grand prix winner then they deserved to reap the benefit. But Prost did not insist on such a commitment, something for which Jenson and his management team would be eternally grateful.

Button flew back from a holiday in Mexico to test the Prost, taking over the programme from regular team driver Jean Alesi, himself no mean F1 performer. The young Englishman adapted immediately and seamlessly to the challenge of operating a 3-litre grand prix car. He was instantly on the pace, handling the Prost with a decisive familiarity that had the pit crew mentally confused for a few seconds, almost forgetting that

Alesi hadn't in fact stayed on to continue driving the car for another day.

The figures were impressive. Alesi had lapped in a best time of 1min 14.8sec after two days of testing at Barcelona. Then Jenson had a day to himself running with a comparable fuel load to that used when the Frenchman had been running. He was also using the

tyres Alesi had used the previous day. Encouraged simply to go out and find his feet, Jenson was told that if he got into the 1min 28sec bracket by the end of the day, he would be doing well. Within five flying laps he'd done a 1min 26.8sec. He came into the pit lane and had a think about things. Then he did another six lap run and topped it off with a 1min 24.4sec best.

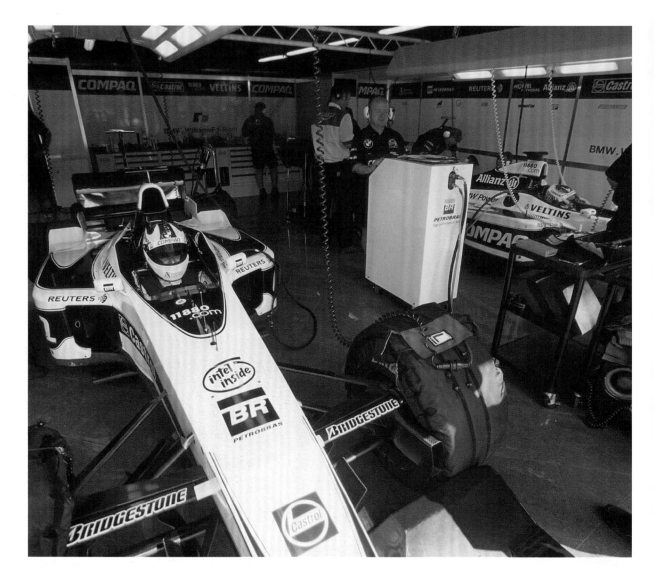

Seasoned engineer Humphrey Corbett was working for Prost on Button's car that day and was dazzled by what he saw. 'I can remember being incredibly impressed at the end of the day,' said Corbett in 2004, by which time he was working as race engineer on the Toyota TF104 being raced by Olivier Panis. 'Immediately he was within a second of our regular driver Jean Alesi. We thought "Bloody hell, who is this guy?" He wasn't flustered, he was so relaxed and his feedback was very good. It was as if the guy had driven F1 for five years.'

Yet although Button was impressive, Prost had other problems on his hands simply keeping the team afloat.

Stressful moment. Button and Junqueira side by side in the Williams-BMW garages during their crucial battle for the vacant seat. (LAT)

Jenson accelerates out of the pits at Barcelona during his pre-season test for Williams. It was a close call, but he got the job! (LAT)

Cashflow rather than promising young drivers was the real priority. So Jenson watched and waited, wondering whether he might not have to complete a second year in Formula 3 in order to consolidate his reputation. His anxiety was heightened very slightly when he heard that Darren Manning had been approached by Williams after winning the two end-of-season F3 classics in Macau and Korea, races in which Button chased him home to post a couple of second places. As Jenson told David Tremayne, by this stage it almost seemed as though he'd become the victim of his own success. Ignoring the fact that Manning had benefited from a powerful Toyota engine in those two Far East races, if Button was so clever, said the logic, then this chap Manning must be even better. But there was more to it than that. Williams had met Darren before when he'd

been short-listed for a Renault drive in the BTCC with Williams Touring Car Engineering, so he was already on Frank's radar screen.

The F1 grapevine is always alert, alive and vibrant. Within days of Button's test in the Prost the gossip began to do the rounds. David Robertson phoned Jim Wright, the Williams team's marketing director, with news of the Prost test. Wright was impressed, but wanted to be sure of the details before he communicated the facts to Frank Williams. Frank wasn't an easy man to impress and any hint that a third party might be hustling him into a deal had historically been met with indifference. One only had to look at his track record. In 1992 he'd run out of patience and withdrawn from further negotiations with the newly crowned World Champion Nigel Mansell. That decision led to Mansell leaving F1 and moving to

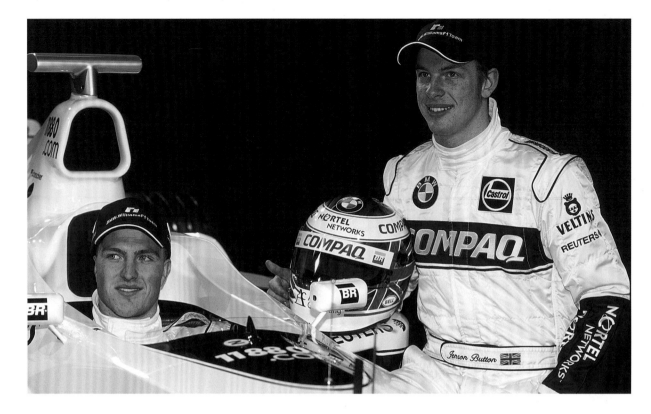

the US where he won the CART championship the following year. Four years later, in 1996, Frank similarly withdrew from negotiations with Damon Hill for an extension of the British driver's contract as Hill was poised to win the title. Williams felt he was being hustled and responded accordingly.

A couple of weeks later Frank telephoned the young British driver. Jenson could hardly believe what he was hearing when he received a telephone call from Frank Williams expressing interest in his services. 'I was having a drink with a few friends just before Christmas when my mobile rang and the voice at the end of the line said it was Frank Williams,' he said. 'I immediately suspected it was somebody playing a joke, but Frank said he just wanted to touch base with me and he later 'phoned back with the offer of a test drive.'

Frank had already done a great deal of homework. He'd telephoned Harald Huysman at his office in Oslo and quizzed him in great detail about the Prost test, running through the whole thing almost lap by lap. In particular, he wanted to be sure about the fuel load

Ralf tries the Williams FW22 cockpit for size at the official launch of the FW22 in January 2000, as Jenson, looking a little stilted in this official snap, stares into the middle distance. (LAT)

My turn now. Button slips into the FW22 cockpit at the official launch as everybody else grins broadly in support. (LAT)

Jenson had been running as that was the true key to the comparative performance against Alesi. If it transpired that Jenson had been running with a lighter car than the Frenchman, the comparison would have been distorted. If Williams was going to give Button a test run, he had to be sure. Huysman corroborated all the initial evidence. The signs were that Jenson's performance had been geuinely spectacular. As a result, on 13 January 2000, Jenson arrived at the Jerez circuit in southern Spain. He would have a run in the interim Williams FW21B development car. It had one of the previous year's chassis which had raced with a Supertec engine installed but now equipped with one of the first of the new BMW E41 V10s.

Williams was impressed with Button's personality, but decided to check out those impressions with BMW's newly appointed competitions manager Gerhard Berger. Gerhard confessed that he judged Button an interesting character and was keen to give him a run. But he was more impressed than even he could ever have anticipated after Jenson's first test at Jerez.

'What you've got to remember is that I knew Jerez extremely well, having driven my last grand prix there in 1997,' he said, 'so I knew instantly what I was looking for when I went up to the top of the control tower and watched Jenson lapping the circuit.

'It was quite incredible. He'd not driven an F1 car before, but he was instantly on the line, never ran wide, and the only indication that he was pushing hard came from the occasional locked brake as he probed the limit. It was obvious that he was an instinctive driver.'

Yet to some extent the Jerez test was inconclusive. The new BMW engine wasn't reliable enough to give the new boy a sufficiently consistent run to be able to come to a fair conclusion. Yet time constraints were crowding in on the Williams team. The launch of the new Williams-BMW FW22, together with the team's new sponsorship package from Compaq, was due to be unveiled to the press at Barcelona on 24 January. But there was another driver in the frame for the drive, a young Brazilian called Bruno Junqueira. The sponsorship link between the Brazilian fuel company Petrobras and Williams had brought Junqueira into the Grove camp as a test driver. He had also made quite a name for himself in the 1999 Formula 3000 championship, which was won by the German driver Nick Heidfeld.

As the *Autocourse* annual recorded in its annual review written by Simon Arron, 'Brazilian Bruno Junqueira (Petrobras) is already favoured to succeed Heidfeld after a slightly rough-and-tumble season that underlined his searing pace and adventurous racecraft. His lone win, at Hockenheim, was just reward after he zipped past team-mate Max Wilson at about 170mph, with two wheels on the grass. It was one hell of a move and, to many, he was the revelation of the season. A few too many scrapes scotched his title chances, but it was an impressive year nonetheless.'

Once the decision had been made to ditch Zanardi, it was inevitable that Junqueira would be a candidate for the vacant drive. Bruno was more experienced than Button, but there seemed little doubt that the British F3 graduate would offer more long-term potential. Even so, it was a risk. The pressure ramped up on the two men when Frank Williams decided the only way to

Facing the press. Jenson gets a taste of what life is going to be like from now on as he is interviewed by the F1 media pack at the start of his spell as a Williams driver. (LAT)

Ralf Schumacher accepted Jenson's arrival at Williams with good grace. He would be less amused when Jenson put him under huge pressure in the second half of the 2000 season (LAT)

resolve the situation was a 'shoot out' between the two men at the Circuit de Catalunya on 23 January, the eve of the official announcement.

Jim Wright, the Williams team's head of marketing, takes up the story. 'It was obviously going to be close because while Jenson had obviously been impressive in the Prost test, Junqueira was a very good driver, very quiet and methodical, and he'd already had a fair deal of mileage in the car,' he recalled. 'But come the shoot-out there was precious little to choose between them. The lap times were pretty well identical. Frank came onto me and said "We can't make a decision. We need more time. It's just too close between them. You'll only be able to announce Ralf as one confirmed driver tomorrow and we'll just have to explain that the second driver will be one of these two other guys."

'So we got ourselves organised to do just that, complete with supplies of media packs on both Jenson and Bruno and that was how we were going to do it.

Then on the morning of the announcement, Frank called me from his car on the way into the circuit, with just 15 minutes left before the media conference was scheduled to begin and said "Jimmy, we've decided to go with Jenson". So it is absolutely true that Jenson didn't know until ten minutes before the announcement. But Frank absolutely insisted on seeing Bruno first to explain that he hadn't got the drive, but it had been very close, and that he would be giving him a test driving contract.'

Junqueira continued in F3000 through the 2000 season and ended up winning the championship. He contained his disappointment over not getting the Williams drive pretty well, even though he eventually had to switch to the CART series in North America to sustain his career in the longer term. 'Racing in Formula 1 has always been my dream,' he said during the summer of 2000. 'That's not something I want to give up on. But as the season went on, more and more people kept saying to me "Look, you might be better off trying to do something else if there are no decent drives available". The more I thought about it, the more I began to see their point of view.'

So Frank made his decision in Button's favour on the day of the official unveiling of the Williams FW22. BBC Radio Five Live radio commentator Jonathan Ledgard recalls being beckoned over for a word with Frank only minutes before the official announcement was due to be made.

The popular and enthusiastic Ledgard thought he was about to get the scoop of the F1 season, albeit by only a few minutes. He squatted down close to Williams's face. 'Tell me, Jonathan,' asked Frank with some gravitas, 'when is the BBC going to get rid of Alan Hansen from its football commentaries? I can't understand a word he says . . .'

Jenson got the drive and immediately began to

Early setback. In an effort to put in some miles on the all-new Williams-BMW FW22 in good weather conditions, the team went testing at Johannesburg's Kyalami circuit in February 2000. Here Jenson looks pensive after parking up in a gravel trap. (LAT)

But it wasn't supposed to rain at Kyalami. Jenson splashes through an unexpected shower at the former South African Grand Prix venue. (LAT)

impress most observers with his obvious talent. Yet he was under absolutely no illusions. There had been no prevaricating whatsoever on Frank's part. Jenson knew that he would have to perform sensationally well if he was going to keep Juan-Pablo Montoya out of the Williams line-up.

The decision to plump for Montoya for 2001 was eventually formalised at around the time of the Monaco Grand Prix where Frank played absolutely straight with Jenson. He'd signed the young British driver on a five-year contract, so now it was a question of which team he would 'sub let' Button out to for the next few years. It turned out to be the Benetton – soon to be Renault – F1 squad.

Making his reputation. Jenson at speed in the Williams-BMW FW22 during his freshman F1 season. (LAT)

one year to prove it

Williams was a team in transition at the start of the 2000 season. The great days of their partnership with Renault, which had delivered four Drivers' World Championships between 1992 and 1997, were now disappearing in their personal rear-view mirrors. They had spent the 1998 and 1999 seasons wrestling with leased Supertec V10 engines – fixed specification versions of the once-great Renault V10s – but now they

Countdown to his first F1 race. Jenson sits with Williams technical director Patrick Head in the paddock at Melbourne prior to the 2000 Australian Grand Prix at Melbourne. (LAT)

had cut a fresh deal with BMW, an in-depth technical collaboration designed to endure on a long-term basis.

'In September 1999 we produced an FW21B development car for the new engine,' explained Williams Technical Director Patrick Head. 'This basically had the suspension from the 1999 car (the FW21) and the "Step 3" version of the new BMW engine, which was installed in the chassis with the oil tank ahead of the engine rather than in with the gearbox. This produced an oil system problem which, in fact, had a relatively simple solution but took a bit of time to sort out as it only arose when the engine was installed in the car rather than operating on the dynamometer.'

The new FW22 was ready well ahead of the first race of the season, its design philosophy being to flatter the strong points of the FW21. At the same time Head's team had worked hard to eliminate some of its areas of weakness, most notably its poor aerodynamic performance on low downforce circuits. To get the best out of the new BMW type E4 engine it was also fitted with a seven-speed longitudinal gearbox rather than the six-speed transmission used on the 1999 car.

Of course, such considerations were almost of secondary importance to Jenson as the bare fact was that he was now an F1 driver. Sitting strapped in his FW22 as he waited in the pit lane at Melbourne on 10 March, poised to start first practice for the Australian Grand Prix, if he found it hard to take everything in, he certainly concealed any mounting apprehension.

Suddenly the signal was given and he was accelerating out onto the circuit close behind Michael Schumacher, one of his great heroes, at the wheel of his scarlet Ferrari. Yet the sun went in abruptly. Jenson spun into the wall during that Friday free practice session. Frank Williams accepted the new boy's slip with impassive equanimity. He appreciated the pressures

An unfortunate moment. Jenson spun into the wall during first practice for his maiden grand prix. Fortunately, the rumpled Williams FW22 was repairable. (LAT)

Lights, camera, action. Jenson speeds past the Melbourne pits early on in the 2000 Australian Grand Prix. He retired after 46 laps with engine failure. (LAT)

involved. But that didn't alter the fact that Frank and Patrick Head had a deeply ingrained sense of disapproval when it came to drivers – particularly young and inexperienced drivers – crashing their cars.

On the second day things didn't get any better for Jenson. He had to abandon his repaired race car due to fuel pressure problems. Instead, he took over the spare Williams FW22, but a 'red flag' period scuppered his qualifying efforts. He would line up for his first grand prix start 21st on the grid. Only the little known Argentine driver Gaston Mazzacane would be behind him in the struggling Minardi M02.

At the end of the race he would be moderately satisfied. Not with his result, of course, because he failed to finish due to an engine failure after 46 of the race's 56 laps. But it had been a bold and confident debut.

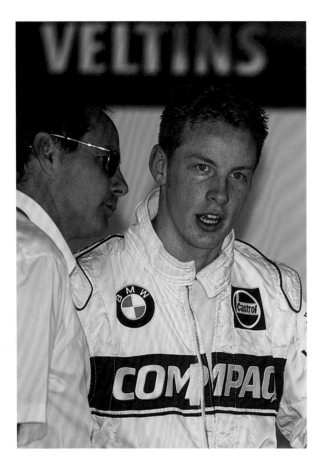

With Gerhard Berger at Melbourne, 2000. The former Ferrari and McLaren driver watched Button's early F1 tests with Williams in Spain and was instantly impressed with the young British driver's precision. (LAT)

Legendary TV Commentator Murray Walker chats with Jenson's father. John Button later received a memorable 60th birthday present from his son – a classic 1950s Chevrolet Corvette sports car! (LAT)

Jenson had driven very tidily, making up places during a fraught opening lap to come round in 15th place.

'My start wasn't the best in the world,' said Button, 'but some people made worse getaways so it wasn't too bad. My first lap was very hectic and I tried to stay out of trouble. It was a nice steady race apart from a little mistake on the fifth lap. I just wish it had lasted another 20 laps.'

The second round of the championship took place at Sao Paulo's ramshackle Interlagos circuit on 25 March. The momentum seemed with him. He qualified ninth, two places ahead of his more seasoned team-mate Ralf Schumacher. He achieved this despite the need for an engine change between the Saturday morning free practice session and qualifying. Jenson was clearly getting the hang of the Formula 1 business.

In the race he would excel again, scoring his first championship point for sixth place after David Coulthard's McLaren-Mercedes was excluded from second place behind Michael Schumacher's winning Ferrari due to an infringement of the rules relating to the car's front wing endplates.

It was the overall quality of Jenson's driving which again attracted attention rather than the seventh place finish, which was magically transformed into sixth through circumstances beyond his own control. He'd fluffed his start, dropping from ninth to 14th by the end of the opening lap, but from then on it was a case of onwards and upwards.

For many laps Jenson was locked in a wheel-to-wheel battle with the highly experienced Jos Verstappen's Arrows A21, eventually slicing a confident path ahead of the Dutchman on lap 56. It was a small, but significant step along the road to Button's maturity. Here on that bumpy undulating circuit that had given so much to F1 history, where memories of epic days

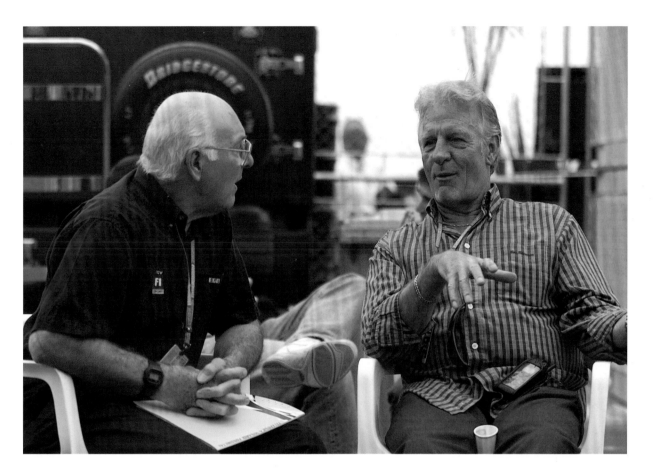

involving the Fittipaldi brothers, Carlos Pace, Ayrton Senna and many, many more, Jenson scored his first crucial championship point. Even at this early stage, it was clear that it wouldn't be his last.

The main rump of the European F1 season was next on the agenda, that helter-skelter of intense racing which starts in the early spring and runs pretty well through to the end of September. This is a particularly high pressure period for the competing teams as the relentless inevitability of the racing schedule makes it extremely demanding when it comes to developing the cars. The Williams-BMW FW22 was very much an experimental car in an experimental season. Williams and the German car manufacturer had been working behind the scenes for a couple of years, but there was nothing like proper race action to highlight the weaknesses within the new alliance.

For the San Marino Grand Prix at Imola things were

looking up, at least for Ralf Schumacher. He qualified his FW22 fifth fastest in 1min 25.871sec. That was a second shy of Mika Häkkinen's pole position with the McLaren-Mercedes MP4/15, but it wasn't a bad show considering just how young the Williams-BMW partnership really was. Unfortunately Jenson made heavy weather of the qualifying session here at the evocatively titled Autodromo Enzo e Dino Ferrari. He couldn't quite get himself into the swing of manhandling his car – brutally, it seemed to him – over the punishing high kerbs. That's all part of the art of squeezing a quick lap out of the Imola circuit and he paid the price by lining up a distant 18th on the grid on 1min 27.135sec.

Jenson's maiden British Grand Prix was always going to be something of an emotional occasion, but to experience that feeling so early in his first F1 season was certainly something of an historic surprise. In 2000 some pseudo-political juggling with the F1 international calendar meant that the race at Silverstone would take place on an unseasonably early Easter Monday rather than its traditional July date when there would have been a chance of much better weather.

As it was, the weather dealt a terrible blow to Button's Silverstone debut. Heavy rain for much of the previous fortnight produced depressing scenes with paying spectators up to their ankles in glutinous mud, their cars bogged down up to their axles. It was all extremely depressing and the public car parks had to be closed on the Saturday in a bid to make things halfway reasonable in time for race morning. On the Sunday morning things got even worse. The combination of a

capacity crowd and the painfully slow process of gaining access to the spectator car parks caused gridlock around the Northamptonshire circuit. Despite warnings from the police not to join the 15-mile traffic jams leading to the circuit, the 60,000-plus crowd displayed remarkable grit and determination. The venue, after all, looked more like the Glastonbury Festival than the British round of a five-star international motorsport.

Once trackside, the sodden fans wanted to be cheered up. Jenson did just that, qualifying a staggering sixth, one place behind Michael Schumacher's Ferrari, but crucially one place ahead of his team-mate Ralf. Come the race the fans were paid back for their

The two Williams-
BMW FW22s in
close formation
during the
unseasonably
early 2000
British Grand Prix
at Silverstone,
held on Easter
Sunday. Ralf and
Jenson finished
fourth and fifth.
(LAT)

Jenson meets his
fans at
Silverstone where
he impressed
everybody in the
paddock with that
fifth place finish.
(LAT)

discomfort and inconvienience. At the head of the pack David Coulthard stormed to an enormously popular win in the McLaren, while Jenson, who'd run ahead of Ralf until the first round of refuelling stops, stormed home fifth. Both FW22s were misfiring badly in the closing stages of the race and, as it subsequently transpired, were remarkably fortunate to make it to the chequered flag. Jenson also produced the seventh fastest lap of the afternoon in what was a very convincing performance.

At the Spanish Grand Prix in Barcelona most of the media focus was on David Coulthard, who had survived a private jet accident the previous week at Lyons airport in which both the pilots died. It was probably just as

well, as Button qualified a disappointing 11th, complaining that his FW22 seemed unduly affected by the crosswinds. Come the race, though, he drove well. He worked his way steadily through to sixth place before hopes of adding to his World Championship points tally were scuppered by an engine failure with four laps to go. Ralf finished fifth.

Button's first visit to Monaco was fraught with difficulties. Williams team insiders were impressed with the assured manner with which he tackled the unforgiving 2.094-mile ribbon of tarmac through some of the most expensive real estate on the planet. But his qualifying effort certainly didn't reflect the obvious energy and poise that was being deployed in the cockpit of Williams's number 10 car. When Eddie Irvine's Jaguar was limping home after suffering power steering failure, the flurry of yellow warning flags saw Jenson ease off the throttle on what he hoped would be his best qualifying lap. He ended up 14th on the grid, five places behind Ralf Schumacher. It wasn't any consolation when he heard Ralf complaining that Irvine had got in his way on his best lap as well.

The race start was dramatic. Initially Pedro Diniz, who had qualified his Sauber C19 in 19th place, was left stranded in the middle of the pack as the field accelerated away on the formation lap. It seemed as though the Brazilian was destined to start from the back of the grid, but as the pack stopped on the grid proper, Alex Wurz's Benetton suffered an engine failure. Race officials immediately aborted the start.

When the race finally got underway, Michael Schumacher's Ferrari accelerated into the lead. But an electrical problem with the race timing computer triggered the 'abort start' procedure and red warning strips appeared on all the teams' timing screens. Unfortunately, red flags weren't immediately waved around the circuit, so the pack roared onwards around what it thought was the opening lap. At the ultra-tight Loews hairpin, Pedro de la Rosa attempted to squeeze his Arrows around the outside of Button's Williams and the end result saw Jenson inadvertently tapping the Spaniard into a spin. The two cars shuddered to a halt, blocking the circuit, and the race was stopped.

Jenson jogged back to the pits to take over the spare Williams FW22. While running in 19th place after 17 laps his first Monaco Grand Prix ended when he pulled into the pits and retired with fluctuating oil pressure.

Button would press Ralf Schumacher pretty hard in

The Ralf and Jenson show. Button couldn't initially match the younger Schumacher's pace, but by the second half of the 2000 season his speed was seriously rattling his more experienced rival. (LAT)

the closing stages of the 2000 season, but it wasn't enough to keep his drive. The shaping of his immediate career prospects had been finalised long before the end of the 2000 season. The team was unquestionably impressed with Juan Pablo Montoya, and Frank was determined to get him on the payroll.

At the 2000 Canadian Grand Prix, David Robertson finally decided that he had to press Frank Williams on the issue of whether or not Jenson would be kept on the BMW Williams race team the following year.

'Yes, we went into the Williams deal knowing there was a possibility that Montoya would be considered for 2001, but we negotiated an agreement to take care of that and it was the first time it had been done,' he said. 'If you talk to all these teams now you'll find, for example, teams like Renault have an interest in the driver. Frank had to pay him until he no longer wanted him, so knowing that he was going to take Montoya on he still paid Jenson and we were able to negotiate for his [Jenson's] salary elsewhere, which was a unique situation.

'Jenson wanted to stay with Williams, but I knew Frank had this decision to make [about Montoya]. But he was reluctant to tell me. So I went direct to him and said "Frank, please tell me, am I free to talk to another team?" He told me I could, so I knew that the deal was done. So from then on I went out and made myself busy, basically.'

While the astute Roberston was formulating the next step in his negotiating strategy, Button had a disappointing Canadian Grand Prix. Bugged by fuel pick-up problems he qualified a distant 18th. In the race itself, he trailed home 11th.

Frank Williams made the dilemma clear. 'We had the choice between Jenson and Juan Pablo,' he explained.

'But we inclined towards Juan simply because he'd spent two years in 900bhp Indycars and was further down his career development path than Jenson, if you like. In any case, we would have lost our option on his services if we hadn't taken up the chance of bringing him back to the F1 team. He knew that, Jenson knew that and it certainly wasn't a negative reflection on Jenson. He just didn't have the experience to match Juan Pablo, but he was clearly hugely talented.'

After their trip across the Atlantic, the F1 teams returned to Europe to pick up the threads of the championship programme. The next race was the Austrian Grand Prix at the A1-Ring where the Michelin-shod Williams FW22s demonstrated their aversion to low-grip track surfaces. Button and Ralf Schumacher qualified 18th and 19th. In the race Button kept out of trouble to finish in an excellent fifth place, only just losing out in a battle for fourth with Jacques Villeneuve's BAR-Honda. He would come to know a lot more about Villeneuve in the years ahead.

'It was a hard race,' said Jenson. 'The first corner was pretty tough to find a way through and I'm not sure how I came out of it at the end. The team did a good job with my pit stop, but unfortunately Jacques was just able to pop out of the pits ahead of me.'

By this time there was much media speculation that Button would be dropped by Williams at the end of the season. On the face of it, this was another case of Frank Williams getting shot of Britain's latest F1 super-hero in the same way as he'd apparently ditched the legendary Nigel Mansell at the end of 1992. But, of course, there was more to this business than met the eye.

The subtleties of Jenson's contract had not been shared with the media and the situation looked slightly confused, certainly from the touchlines. In a sense this was compounded by what some observers saw as a mid-season dip in Jenson's performance. In reality, this was a by-product of his over-ambitious experimentation with his car's set-up combined with the fact that BMW had detuned its V10 engines in the interests of mechanical longevity.

But at Hockenheim, Jenson got his personal development curve back on track. Despite having to start the German Grand Prix from the back of the grid after his car refused to fire up prior to the formation lap, he stormed through to fourth at the chequered flag. This flawless drive was strategically abetted by two perfectly timed stops on laps 27 and 34, making the switch to rain tyres on the second pit visit.

'The team made an excellent job calling me in at the right time to switch to wet tyres,' said Jenson. 'It was very difficult to drive at that moment, because at the back of the circuit it was dry and in the pit lane it was raining. It was also a very exciting moment when I passed Mika Salo's Sauber to take fourth just two laps from the end of the race.'

Patrick Head, seldom easily impressed, added, 'It was a brilliant result for Jenson.' It was also timely. At the Hungarian Grand Prix a fortnight later it was confirmed that he would, after all, be staying in F1 for the 2001 season, with the Renault team.

By the middle of August 2000, Jenson's F1 future for the next two seasons had been successfully secured. David Robertson finalised a deal with Flavio Briatore for him to drive alongside Giancarlo Fisichella in the Benetton F1 squad starting with the first race of 2001. The arrangement gave Williams the option to claim him back as one of their race drivers for 2003 if Frank and Patrick Head felt so inclined.

Button radiated confidence when quizzed about his planned move. 'I felt Benetton offered me the best opportunity of doing what I want above all else, to win races,' he said. 'I genuinely believe that Benetton will be challenging for victories over the next couple of seasons because I know what it has planned. I am fully aware of its commitment, and it certainly has the people, skill and resources to be successful. I will do my best to repay Flavio for the faith he has shown in me. If that means beating Williams in the process, so be it. Frank Williams would expect no other attitude from me.'

Briatore, a hard nosed wheeler dealer who had helped shape Michael Schumacher's early career with Benetton, had been impressed with Button during his freshman year in F1. Privately, though, he was a little concerned with Jenson's image as a bit of a playboy. This derived largely from the image of him schmoozing his close pals on his luxury yacht 'Little Missie', which was moored alongside the paddock during the 2000

Monaco Grand Prix weekend. Yet Briatore was astute enough to see past that. He knew that Jenson had talent and could understand that a young man suddenly propelled into this world of wealth and conspicuous consumption would be keen to have a good time.

'He's motivated and this is a big chance for him,' Briatore told *Autosport*. There will be a new Renault engine [for 2001] and we want to be more competitive. With Giancarlo Fisichella and Jenson we have a nice combination, two young and ambitious drivers.'

Frank Williams added wistfully, 'There is no doubt in my mind that Jenson will go on to be a truly great grand prix driver. He has astonished the Williams team with his immediate grasp of Formula 1 and the calmness of his approach.'

Quizzed on whether Button might have it in him to win races, or even a World Championship with Renault, Briatore was more cautious. 'Many people have asked that question,' he said, 'but we will not be ready to win the world championship next year. Races, I do not know. To do that you need to have a car that is on the first or second row [of the grid] at least 60 per cent of the time. In 2001, we will try to be really competitive and win races regularly in 2002.'

Making progress in Formula 1 is very like making progress through life in general. You take your chances when the opportunities present themselves. You benefit or suffer setbacks from the judgements and decisions made by others. The real trick is to engineer the situation to be in the right place, with the right team, at the most advantageous moment.

Consider David Coulthard in 1995. He drove the first part of the season with a tonsil infection that knocked the stuffing out of him. By the second half of the season he had recovered both his health and his racing form, and won the Portuguese Grand Prix at Estoril. But by then Williams had already lost him to McLaren-Mercedes for the 1996 season. It wasn't just because they wanted to replace him with Jacques Villeneuve, more because David already had a contract with McLaren even before the start of the 1995 season.

So what is the point of all this? Well, Damon Hill won the 1996 World Championship in a Williams-Renault while Coulthard struggled with an uncompetitive

Jenson meets a
couple of his
young fans away
from the
racetrack, this
time in Bath
during the
summer of
2000. (LAT)

McLaren. Would Coulthard, who some insiders believe was quicker than Hill, have won the 1996 title had he remained with Williams? Possible, but who can say?

In a similar fashion, if Button had shown a touch more speed in the first half of 2000, or Montoya hadn't won the Indy 500, perhaps Frank Williams would have retained the Englishman for 2001. In such circumstances he'd have got his hands on the much-improved Williams-BMW FW23 and perhaps posted his maiden grand prix win. After all, the FW23 won four races shared between Montoya and Ralf Schumacher. But by that time Jenson would be trapped in the cockpit of what turned out to be an uncompetitive Benetton.

For the moment, however, he had the remainder of the 2000 season to complete. After Hockenheim came Jenson's first visit to the Hungaroring, the tortuous little circuit 20km outside of Budapest that has hosted the Hungarian GP since 1986. Ralf and Jenson qualified fourth and eighth, helped by aerodynamic revisions and an upgraded engine specification. Ralf finished fifth, but a throttle control problem caused Jenson to lose power in the closing stages, dropping him back behind Jarno Trulli's Jordan and Eddie Irvine's Jaguar to post a ninth place finish. 'Jenson drove an amazingly good defensive race,' said Patrick Head. 'Certainly I think he might have been in the points if he hadn't had that problem.'

Then came the Belgian Grand Prix at Spa-Francorchamps, that epic track through the pine forests in the south-east of the country, close to the German border. In qualifying, Jenson was simply scintillating, laying the Williams-BMW into the long corners with a measured precision that reminded Patrick Head of Alain Prost's smooth driving style when he drove for the team in 1993 and won his fourth World Championship.

While Mika Häkkinen's McLaren-Mercedes took pole ahead of Jarno Trulli's Jordan, Button stunned the watching pit lane by edging out Michael Schumacher's Ferrari to place his Williams third on the starting grid. 'I am absolutely ecstatic,' he said. 'I thought I could only outqualify Michael Schumacher if he had gone out or fallen off the track or something.'

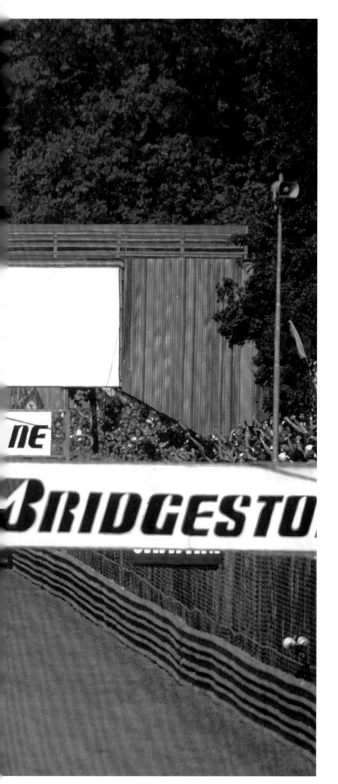

Lurid moment.
Jenson lurches
off the track
onto the grass
and is about to
glance the barrier
during an
unfortunate
incident behind a
slow-running pack
prior to the
restart of the
2000 Italian
Grand Pix. (LAT)

On the morning of the race heavy rain doused the circuit but it stopped well before the scheduled start time. Still, it was decided that the contest should start behind the safety car as there was still a considerable amount of standing water. At the end of the opening lap the safety car pealed into the pits with Häkkinen 0.8sec ahead of Trulli and Button, and that's how they remained. Mika stretched his advantage all the while, until lap four when Jenson got a bit out of shape under braking for the 'Bus stop' chicane before the pits and Schumacher nipped by into third.

Anxious to make up for his slip, Jenson tucked in behind the Ferrari. As Michael dived inside Trulli at the tight La Source hairpin, he tried to follow but ended up hitting the Jordan and spinning it out of the race. Trulli was not amused. 'I think Jenson was a bit too aggressive too soon,' he said. 'He should have waited for a couple of laps as he would have probably got past me since I was struggling slightly. There was not enough room for Jenson to overtake as well as Schumacher, so he hit me.'

After the promise of the opening laps, Button survived to finish a disappointing sixth on a day when Mika Häkkinen brilliantly caught and passed Michael Schumacher's Ferrari to post what many regarded as the greatest victory of his F1 career. Ralf Schumacher was third in the other Williams-BMW, separated from Button by David Coulthard's fourth placed McLaren.

The Italian Grand Prix at Monza rounded off the European season as usual. But the race will be remembered for the multiple pile-up at the second chicane on the opening lap. This triggered a storm of flying debris, a piece of which killed a trackside marshal, 30-year-old Paolo Ghislimberti. With cars scattered in all directions, the safety car was called out to lead the field slowly round while the track was cleared.

The safety car's flashing lights were turned off on lap 11, signalling to the field that it would be pulling into the pits at the end of that lap. In preparation for the resumption of racing, Schumacher slowed suddenly as he came down towards the right-hand Parabolica turn in an attempt to warm up his brakes and tyres after miles of running at below race speed. The cars in the queue behind braked hard and Jenson, running sixth, suddenly found himself faced with the back of Giancarlo Fisichella's slowing Benetton, and he lurched onto the grass to avoid a collision.

A glancing impact with the barrier damaged his Williams's suspension and he slid off at the next corner, ending up in the gravel trap. Michael later apologised,

but Jenson was not amused. 'I am very annoyed,' he said. 'I got told off for overtaking under the safety car, but I think I avoided quite a big accident. Jacques Villeneuve [a few cars ahead in the queue] stood on the brakes so as not to overtake the people in front, but I had nowhere to go and just missed a marshal standing at the side of the track.'

So that was the end of Jenson Button's first Italian Grand Prix. He would also retire from the inaugural US Grand Prix at Indianapolis with an engine failure. But finished a superb fifth in the Japanese Grand Prix at Suzuka after qualifying fifth on the grid, one place ahead of Ralf Schumacher. 'My start was quite disastrous,' said Jenson. 'Having started fifth, I dropped back to seventh but just kept pushing. The car was well balanced and worked very well. I was putting in quite

The Williams-BMWs of Jenson and Ralf shadow Michael Schmacher's Ferrari at the La Source hairpin in the 2000 Belgian Grand Prix. (LAT)

Jenson with BMW Motorsport director Mario Theissen in the pits at Sepang. It was a difficult first year for BMW in partnership with Williams, but Theissen quickly formed a high opinion of Jenson's capability. (LAT)

good times, although obviously not as good as Ferrari or McLaren.'

Now he had served his apprenticeship and it was time to leave Williams for the less certain waters of the Renault squad. 'Jenson was really the discovery of the year,' said Frank Williams. 'I don't think anybody would deny that. He was very popular in the team, and both his driving talent and his potential spoke for themselves.'

'Jenson was excellent,' added Patrick Head. 'He probably had a few more engine problems early in the season compared with Ralf, but he was a quick learner and adapted well to the challenge of circuits which were unfamiliar to him. In short, he was almost perfect. Jenson also rattled Ralf's cage and he didn't like it one bit.'

Down to earth with a bump. 15th place for Renault in the 2001 British Grand Prix was a sad contrast to 5th the previous year. (LAT)

learning about renault

Although Frank Williams had a long-term option on Button's services, he effectively blessed his move to Benetton-Renault in 2001 where he would be partnered by Giancarlo Fisichella. He had a tough time integrating with the team, largely because there had been so much expectation surrounding his efforts the previous year. Now he was just another young driver wrestling with an undeveloped car. His lack of seasoning was about to show, perhaps more than at any time in his career.

The ethos at Benetton was different to that prevailing within most contemporary F1 teams. In a sense the contrast with Williams couldn't have been greater. Like Williams it was underpinned by solid engineering and an ingrained competitive spirit. But while Williams and Patrick Head were unashamed petrol heads, Benetton's team principal Flavio Briatore was made of very different stuff. Part businessman, part playboy, he'd gained a reputation for working hard and playing harder. Whether it was spending time at his luxury estate in Kenya, lolling on a yacht in the Mediterranean or wandering the pit lane at Monte Carlo, Briatore cut a very different figure to that which the F1 establishment was used to dealing with.

Since entering the Forumla 1 arena in 1989, Briatore had also developed into one of the most astute and influential of all the F1 powerbrokers. In a sense, as he freely admitted, it was because he was not a motorsport fan and could therefore slip the sport's problems into a wider focus than some of his more established colleagues. Flavio was an entrepreneur, a wheeler dealer. He believed that F1 should be glamorous, spectacular and connected with the wider TV-viewing public. He didn't regard it as a niche pastime aimed at the dyed-in-the-wool enthusiast.

'When I first came into Formula 1 in 1989 [as Benetton team principal], it was really a game for engineers,' he said. 'It was a battle for technology. But it always seemed to me that we were rather missing the point. Here was a huge international show, a global televised event, yet … nobody seemed to be thinking about their public.' Briatore had worked on the Milan stock exchange in the early 1970s at a time when the Benetton clothing empire was starting its spectacular growth. In 1979 the Treviso-based company opened its first five stores in the US; three years later Briatore took charge of their marketing operation across the Atlantic.

In 1989 Luciano Benetton asked him to look at their struggling Formula One team. He went to the Australian Grand Prix, looked at it through a shopkeeper's eyes and took the job as team principal. 'I entered Formula One from a different background, a different area,' he said. 'When I came into the sport, my colleagues, the people around me, had been breathing the Formula One exhaust fumes for many years. My first impression was that there was a huge fascination about the Formula One business. But why weren't we taking advantage of that? And why wasn't it possible to put

Jenson visits the *Autosport* show at the NEC early in January 2001 and does a little impromptu promotional work for *F1 Racing* magazine. (LAT)

Benetton drivers (from left); Jenson, Giancarlo Fisichella, Fernando Alonso and Mark Webber. (LAT)

on such a good show at half the price? Our product is incredibly expensive and the customer doesn't understand why it is so expensive.

'I knew nothing at all about Formula One before I came into the sport. But my commercial schooling was with Benetton, a very aggressive company. For us, the product was super important, because we were selling millions of items. But the marketing was also very important as well. But in Formula One, nobody was talking about marketing or lifestyle. Only technology, technology, technology.'

If Jenson had any doubts that Briatore was different, he had only to wait for the official launch of the Benetton B201-Renault. It took place in the dramatic surroundings of St Mark's Square in the middle of Venice with hundreds of the world's motorsport media flown in specially for the occasion and transported from Venice airport in a flotilla of chartered cruisers.

'I want Jenson because I believe what he has done this year in his first season has been quite impressive,' Flavio told *Autosport*. 'I never saw him make any big

mistakes in the race or fail to finish because of his own error, even though he has been racing on some circuits that he did not know before. And if you look at how he went at Silverstone, which he knew well, he was very quick. I think the guy is good. I hope we can give him a competitive car and we'll see what happens. He's young and nice for Formula One. He's good with the sponsors and the public. He needs to be more aggressive, but that is part of experience.'

Renault's purchase of the Benetton team at the start of the 2000 season was part of a long-term project to mesh the French car maker's pedigree as a leading-edge F1 engine specialist with Benetton's high-tech chassis capability. In 2000, the team had used a Supertec V10, derived from the engine used in Jacques Villeneuve's 1997 World Championship-winning Williams. But for 2001 the team switched to an all-new 111° V10 developed by Jean-Jacques His and his team at Renault Sport.

It would prove to be a disappointing season for Jenson. His team-mate Giancarlo Fisichella would outqualify

At the official launch of the Benetton B201 in Venice, 6 February 2001, together with Flavio Briatore and Luciano Benetton. (LAT)

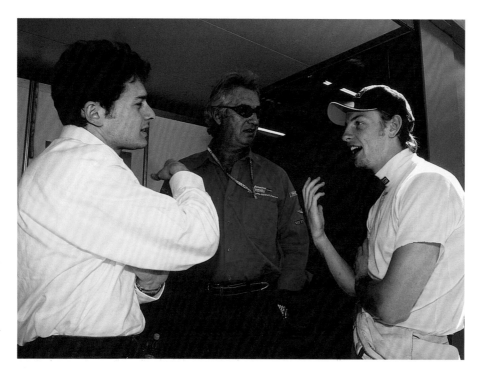

A new beginning. In the pits at Melbourne prior to the 2001 Australian Grand Prix together with new team-mate Giancarlo Fisichella and Benetton team principal Flavio Briatore. (LAT)

him 13–4 over the course of the year and looked a more convincing operator than the young British driver. 'In my view, Fisichella was quicker than Jenson's previous team-mate Ralf Schumacher at Williams,' said Mike Gascoyne, Renault's technical director, 'and that made it difficult for him and he had to work hard to adapt. He knuckled down in the second half of the year and got his head down much better once we had a two-car test team up and running.'

As usual, the 2001 season opened with the Australian Grand Prix at Melbourne's splendid Albert Park circuit. Twelve months after all the media interest surrounding Jenson's debut for Williams, the attention switched to his successor, the Indy 500 winner Juan Pablo Montoya. In the Benetton camp, life looked stressful and difficult. On the morning of qualifying, Jenson's car needed a gearbox change while Fisichella's B201 developed a water leak. They qualified 16th and 17th, well off the pace.

Come the race, things could hardly have gone worse for Jenson. He incurred a 10-second stop–go penalty after the stewards judged that his mechanics had remained too long on the starting grid prior to the

formation lap. Later in the race, with just six laps to go, a broken exhaust caused the wiring loom to burn through, and forced Jenson to retire. He withdrew from the contest almost unnoticed.

It was difficult to know where to look for reassurance. In Malaysia they were 16th and 17th on the grid, both drivers struggling for grip and handling balance, but this time Fisichella was fractionally ahead. In the race, Jenson was once again little more than a footnote, trailing home 11th. It was difficult to see how it could get any worse. But in Brazil, on the Autodromo Jose Carlos Pace at Interlagos, that's precisely what happened. Beset by oil leaks and a generally dismal performance Fisichella lined up 18th, two places ahead of Button. Button finished 10th, three laps behind David Coulthard's victorious McLaren Mercedes.

But there was nothing they could do in the short-term. Drastic technical compromises were being forced on the team because the new Renault V10 was around 100bhp down on its rivals. It was no joke trying to race the opposition in such circumstances. There were cylinder block problems to be surmounted, but nothing in Formula One can be changed overnight. Major

In Jenson's first race as a Benetton driver, at Melbourne in March 2001, he retired with a broken exhaust with six laps remaining. (LAT)

Struggling around Imola in the 2001 San Marino Grand Prix where a distant 12th place was the only reward for Jenson's efforts. (LAT)

engineering problems take time. It began to look like Button's career was being wrecked on the rocks of Benetton's lack of competitiveness.

'We always knew that the first part of the season would be a problem,' said Gascoyne. 'It would have been all-too-easy to have opted for another season with the old Supertec V10 and we might well have ended up as high as fifth in the World Championship rankings. But the trouble is that we'd have faced the prospect of tackling 2002 in the knowledge that we had little realistic prospect of finishing better than fifth in that year's championship either.

'We had no alternative but to press on as boldly as we could. We had to accept compromises at the start of the season in the hope that we could make progress at the other end of the year. Sure, as racers, it was very frustrating to turn up to those early season races knowing we were going to qualify 18th or 19th. But we really didn't want to waste time on short-term fixes.'

The Benetton top brass might have hoped things would take a turn for the better at the first European race of the season, the San Marino Grand Prix at Imola's Autodromo Enzo e Dino Ferrari. No chance. Jenson crept onto the back of the grid with the 21st fastest time and shared the final row with Tarso Marques in the Minardi. The race turned out to be another one to forget.

On lap 19 Jenson brought the Benetton B201 into the pits from 17th place for what turned out to be a 7.4-second refuelling stop. Unfortunately, a malfunction with the refuelling rig meant that no fuel went into the car and he had to come in again next time around, which dropped him down close to last. Eventually Jenson struggled home in 12th, hampered by his earlier refuelling difficulties and experiencing shoulder strain.

Briatore attempted to put an optimistic gloss on the situation. 'At the moment we are just attempting to survive, but from the French Grand Prix onwards we hope to be upping the power and closing the performance gap,' he said. It sounded like a forlorn hope.

Jenson finished 15th in the Spanish Grand Prix at Barcelona, a truly dreadful showing. He had another oil leak during practice for the Austrian Grand Prix at the A1-Ring, then trailed around at the back in the race after again qualifying on the back row with Tarso Marques. He eventually spun off on his own oil after his engine expired. Thankfully, things improved a touch for Jenson's second visit to Monaco. Mike Gascoyne

Living the good life. Jenson in Monte Carlo, where by 2001 he not only had a flat, but also a yacht in the harbour. (LAT)

Button kept the Benetton out of trouble in Monaco to net seventh place in this most exacting of grand prix races. (LAT)

predicted that the B201's low-speed performance on a track where aerodynamic grip was less of an issue, would give the team a boost.

This certainly proved the case for Fisichella who managed to qualify an excellent tenth. Button was 17th, but come the race their fortunes reversed. 'Fisi' survived one brush with the unyielding guard rail, but came a cropper for a second time and retired from the race with damaged suspension. Jenson finished a solid seventh, lapped by Michael Schumacher's winning Ferrari. He was 28 seconds away from scoring his first championship point at the wheel of a Benetton, that being the distance he trailed Jean Alesi's Prost-Ferrari at the chequered flag.

At the Canadian Grand Prix in Montreal, Benetton should have had both cars equipped with power steering for the first time, but the systems were not ready in time. Jenson at least managed to lift himself off the back row of the grid, but 20th wasn't anything to write home about and after 17 laps he pulled off when his car developed an oil leak. The European Grand Prix at the Nürburgring produced little consolation either. 'Understeer and no grip,' shrugged Button after another disappointing 20th place on the grid. He trailed home 13th, two laps behind Schumacher's victorious Ferrari. The nightmare seemed endless, with precious little in terms of light to be seen flickering at the end of the tunnel.

Finally, at the French Grand Prix, there was some hope in Renault's back yard. They fitted a revised aerodynamic package to the cars as well as a new specification Renault engine, which both drivers judged to be a definite step in the right direction. Fisichella qualified 16th, Jenson 17th, but Button admitted that he hadn't really done himself justice even allowing for the fact that his first run was spoiled by Eddie Irvine's Jaguar spinning in front of him. 'My second run was better,' he said, 'but I'm afraid I mucked up the next two because I was supposed to adjust the differential setting after the second corner. Unfortunately, I forgot to do so on both occasions.'

Again, another wretched race ensued for the Benetton team-mates. Fisichella touched Jos Verstappen's Arrows at the start, and lost a few places in the process. Giancarlo judged that must have done some minor damage as the car felt odder and odder under hard braking as the race progressed. That said, the Italian's day was a whole lot better than Button's whose afternoon ended with a spin into a gravel trap after 68 laps, probably due to engine failure. He was classified 16th, four laps down on the winning Ferrari. 'The engine started to cut out before my second refuelling stop and when I pitted Giancarlo was already there,' said Button. 'Not ideal, but because I had a fuel pressure problem and had no option but to come in at that moment.'

In terms of pure track performance, Jenson's second British Grand Prix passed with more of a whimper than

a bang. As Mika Häkkinen surged to victory for McLaren-Mercedes, Jenson struggled round at the back of the field in his now customary position, creeping past the chequered flag in 15th, again two laps down on the winner. In terms of pit lane credibility, Button had dropped from the radar screen. Formula One is an unforgiving business – you are only as good as your last race, nothing more nor less. The fact that the Benetton B201 was a pretty average piece of equipment at best was almost irrelevant. The truth of the matter was that Fisichella was overshadowing Button in the same car, and that simply wasn't good for the English driver's CV.

At Hockenheim, Fisichella and Button lined up 17th and 18th on the grid for the German Grand Prix after showing precious little in the way of the promise they would unlock for the race. A multiple first corner accident, which saw Luciano Burti's Prost vaulting over Michael Schumacher's Ferrari, and leaving the track surface coated with razor-sharp shards of carbon-fibre,

There was no
repeat of
Jenson's glorious
2000 British
Grand Prix outing
when he returned
to Silverstone
with the
Benetton. He
finished 15th.
(LAT)

Visiting the
Springfield Boys'
Club in East
London in
November 2001.
The club is run
for
underprivileged
youngsters in the
area and has
been supported
by the motor
racing community
for more than 30
years. (LAT)

resulted in the race being red flagged to a halt. After the restart the punishing nature of the circuit, allied with 30°C-plus temperatures, exacted a high toll in terms of mechanical unreliability. Yet on this occasion the two Benettons proved to be bulletproof, touring home fourth and fifth to claim a double helping of World Championship points.

'I drove conservatively in the early stages,' said Fisichella, 'and saved enough fuel to do a slightly longer first stint than planned. When I rejoined, I was ahead of Jenson and things continued to go well, although I ran slightly wide near the end and lost a bit of time.' For his part Button was quick to make the point that the Benettons were hardly makeweights in this particular race. 'My car was very well balanced and I think we were quicker than the Jordans and BARs when we were running the same fuel load,' he said. 'But I had one problem. I pulled my water bottle tube out of my

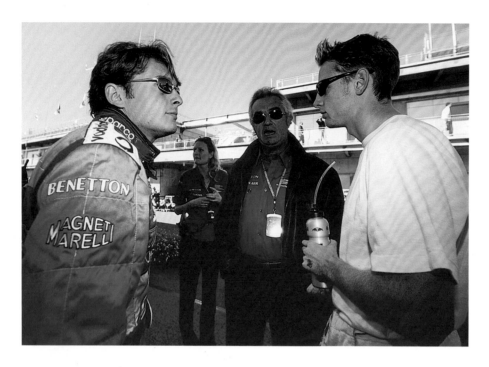

Coming to the end of their partnership, Jenson with team-mate Giancarlo Fisichella at the 2001 US Grand Prix at Indianapolis. The following year Fisi would move to Jordan with Jarno Trulli becoming Jenson's new team-mate. (LAT)

mouth so it was spraying all over my face whenever I braked. It wasn't an easy race, especially with Alesi right behind, but it was good fun.'

Yet the German Grand Prix would only give the Benetton drivers' morale a momentary uplift. In Hungary, Button qualified 17th, collected a 10-second stop–go penalty for an accidental jump start, then spun off the road after 34 laps while running at the tail of the field. Then at Spa-Francorchamps further aerodynamic improvements and another engine upgrade saw Fisichella and Button qualifying sixth and tenth. Giancarlo had demonstrated the effectiveness of the team's launch control system by hurtling down the outside at the start to tuck immediately into second place behind Michael Schumacher's Ferrari.

By the end of the opening lap Fisichella was still hanging on just 3.7 seconds behind Michael, with Rubens Barrichello third in the other Ferrari, and the McLaren-Mercedes of David Coulthard and Mika Häkkinen sandwiching Jenson's Benetton, which was holding fifth place. He was still running fifth on lap 18 when he hit one of the rubber cones delineating the left-hand kerb on the entry to the so-called 'Bus Stop' chicane just before the start line. He skittered on

straight into the wall as the front wing of his Benetton was pulled off. It tucked under the left front wheel, momentarily jamming up the steering.

A fortnight later it looked as though Jenson was about to make up for this slip when he qualified 11th for the Italian Grand Prix at Monza. This was a tense event run under the emotional cloud of the 9/11 terrorist outrage in New York which had taken place the previous week. There were signs of mourning all over the paddock. The Ferraris ran devoid of any sponsorship identification and with black nose cones. The Jaguar airboxes similarly were dressed in black. The Jordans carried the stars and stripes on their airboxes out of respect. Then, on Saturday, the dreadful news filtered through to the track that Alex Zanardi, the popular Italian driver who Button had replaced in the Williams team the previous year, had lost both his legs in a terrible accident during a CART race at the Lausitzring oval circuit near Dresden.

For the jangled, tautly stretched nerves in the Monza paddock, this somehow seemed the last straw on the eve of the grand prix. The Schumacher brothers tried to rally support for a 'no passing' deal until the first two chicanes on the opening lap of the race had been negotiated. This didn't come to anything. Then it was suggested that the race might be started behind the safety car, but that was vetoed by Briatore, BAR boss Craig Pollock and Arrows boss Tom Walkinshaw. They all insisted that their drivers should just get on and do their jobs. 'Briatore is a bully and this is a disgrace,' fumed Jean Alesi.

The race duly went ahead as tempers calmed, but it was to prove a bad day for Button who accidentally slammed into the back of Jarno Trulli's Jordan while braking into the first corner. Trulli was furious. 'Button hit the rear of my car as he turned in and pushed me into a spin,' he said. 'He clearly badly misjudged his braking but I was already in the corner, so there was nothing I could do.'

'I braked at the same time as everybody else,' Jenson apologised, 'but I couldn't stop in time to avoid Trulli. I ran into the back of him, lost my front wing and put him out of the race, for which I was very sorry.' Jenson pitted for repairs, but engine failure claimed him three laps later.

The US Grand Prix at Indianapolis brought better fortune for the Renault squad with Jenson qualifying well with the tenth fastest time, two places ahead of Fisichella. 'It's great to be in the top ten for the first time this year,' he said. 'I just hope this time we can do something at the start and make it round!' He finished ninth, just behind Fisichella, but a lap behind Mika Häkkinen's victorious McLaren.

Finally came Suzuka, and the Japanese Grand Prix, the traditional upbeat finale to the F1 season. Fisichella demonstrated just how formidable Renault's qualifying-spec V10 had become by bagging sixth on the grid, three places ahead of Button. Jenson finished seventh, just missing out on a championship point. But he was on the same lap as Michael Schumacher's victorious Ferrari at the chequered flag, which reflected the progress Benetton had made.

The bottom line for Jenson was 17th place in the World Championship stakes with just those two points from the fifth place at Hockenheim to his credit. His best grid position had been ninth; his worst 21st. He'd now completed 34 Formula One races during which he'd accumulated 14 championship points. Compared with that glorious maiden season with Williams, it all looked rather disappointing. But the upside was that Jenson was adding to his experience. The first season at Benetton had made him tougher, more reslient. Now he had to build on that experience in a bid to make more sense of things in 2002.

Keeping fit in style. Jenson and the Benetton F1 squad training at Malindi in Kenya just before Christmas 2001. (LAT)

A subtle change.
For 2002, Jenson
became a 'works'
Renault driver.
(LAT)

gaining in
stature

Fisichella left for 2002 and Button found himself partnering Jarno Trulli in the Renault squad. Button began to pick up the pace now with excellent fourth places in both Malaysia and Brazil, only losing what would have been his first podium finish at Sepang when he was overtaken by Michael Schumacher on the final lap. Yet now he had to face up to another challenge. Flavio Briatore had decided to replace him for 2003 with his young protégé Fernando Alonso. Jenson had to look for another team.

For the 2002 season, the team's cars were now officially identified as Renault R202s, the Benetton branding now put firmly behind them. As it turned out,

the team would end up fourth in the Constructors' Championship, although the 23 points scored by Button and his new team-mate Jarno Trulli would be collected in dribs and drabs, neither man scoring a single podium finish during the course of the season.

The year started with Renault Sport chairman Patrick Faure confirming that the team would be extremely disappointed if it failed to end up fourth in the championship. The technical programme was again presided over by Mike Gascoyne as technical director and the vastly experienced Pat Symonds in the role of director of engineering. The R202 was powered by a refined version of the wide 111° V10 engine and the

New order. The faces are the same, but the name has changed. Briatore and Button in Melbourne for the start of the 2002 season when the team was officially re-branded under the Renault name.
(LAT)

management very clearly set out its stall with Gascoyne stating that it was Renault's intention 'to win the championship in 2005 and beyond'.

For his part, Jenson started the season in an optimistic frame of mind. Gascoyne, in particular, noticed just how upbeat the British driver had become, successfully shrugging aside the disappointments of the previous season. Trulli, joining the Renault squad after a somewhat bruising spell with Jordan, performed more conservatively in the opening races of the year. It was almost as if he felt he had to take things easy, that easing himself progressively into the routine of a front-line team was the best way in which to recalibrate his own personal performance. That, in part, contributed to Button being the quicker performer in the first half of the year. Later, however, when he knew he would be leaving the team, Button's form would fade slightly. 'Disappointing, but understandable,' said Gascoyne sympathetically.

Ferrari, of course, remained the F1 pace setters. So confident in their own potential, the Maranello brigade arrived in Melbourne for the opening race of the year without bothering to bring their new F2002 challenger. They correctly judged that Michael Schumacher and Rubens Barrichello could still get the job done at this early stage of the season with the previous year's title-winning F2001. Their prime challengers were Kimi Raikkönen and David Coulthard in the new McLaren MP4/17Ds plus Ralf Schumacher and Juan Pablo Montoya in their Williams FW24s. Realistically, the Renault duo could be regarded as 'best of the rest'.

Jenson qualified 11th, four places behind Trulli, but he celebrated the start of his second season with the Briatore brigade by failing to get beyond the first corner of the race. Accelerating away from pole position, Barrichello's Ferrari was hit from behind by Ralf Schumacher's Williams-BMW. As Ralf's car reared up

Trouble ahead.
Fernando Alonso,
Renault's new
test driver, poses
between Trulli and
Button at the
start of the 2002
season. Mid-
season the
Spaniard would be
confirmed as
Jenson's
replacement for
the following year.
(LAT)

The Renault boys
relaxing in
Australia prior to
the opening round
of the 2002
World
Championship.
(LAT)

over the back of the Italian machine it looked for a heart-stopping moment as if it might execute a backward flip. Thankfully the Williams came crashing back down on its wheels and skidded off into the gravel trap at the first turn. In its wake there was mayhem as the pack scattered in all directions.

Jenson was one of the casualties whose race ended there and then. Others out on the spot included Allan McNish's Toyota, Olivier Panis's BAR-Honda, the Saubers of Nick Heidfeld and Felipe Massa, and Giancarlo Fisichella's Jordan. All in all, it was a pretty bad day at the office.

A very different outcome awaited Button in the sweltering heat of Malaysia a fortnight later. There Jenson reported himself quite happy with the handling of his R202, posting an eighth fastest time on his first run. After that he had a slight engine problem and switched to the spare car, which he felt was just as good. By contrast, Trulli wound up a disappointed 12th, unhappy with the balance of his car.

Button ran strongly from the start, avoiding the first

Jenson climbs from his Renault in *parc fermé* at the end of the 2002 Malaysian Grand Prix. To the left is Rubens Barrichello vacating his Ferrari. The Brazilian's team-mate Michael Schumacher passed Jenson for third on the last lap. (LAT)

corner collision between Schumacher's Ferrari and Montoya's Williams, which left Michael trailing into the pits for a replacement nose section to be fitted and Montoya back in 11th. He would be further delayed by the imposition of a drive-through penalty for causing the unscheduled brush between the two cars. Michael rejoined 19th, some 45 seconds behind the leaders and proceeded to drive absolutely flat-out with all the determination and motivation of a first-year F1 novice.

In the closing stages it looked as though Ralf Schumacher, who'd driven a perfect race and kept out

Jenson stretching the legs of the new Renault R202 on his way to a brilliant fourth in the 2002 Brazilian Grand Prix at Interlagos. He started seventh on the grid. (LAT)

Keeping an eye on his mirrors. Button battles to keep David Coulthard's McLaren behind him at Interlagos. The Scot got by to claim third place by 7 seconds at the chequered flag. (LAT)

of trouble on a two-stop strategy, would lead Montoya home for a Williams 1–2 with the team's old boy Jenson joining them on the rostrum. But there was a sting in the race's tail yet to come, much to Button's acute disappointment.

After driving what many people regarded as the finest race of his career, the Renault's rear suspension developed a problem in the closing stages of the race after a tie-rod broke and Michael's Ferrari slipped by on the final lap. 'It was an excellent race for me in spite of the problem at the end,' he said. 'Obviously I'm disappointed not to have got my first podium, but I felt a problem with the suspension two laps from the end and the car began running on three wheels.'

Disappointed though he may have been, Malaysia signalled that the new Renault was a competitive proposition. For the Brazilian Grand Prix at Interlagos, Trulli and Button qualified sixth and seventh after an excellent effort, then vaulted ahead of the two McLarens to run third and fourth behind Michael and Ralf Schumacher by the end of the opening lap. Barrichello soon stormed through to second, but the Renaults kept in touch with both McLarens for much of the race, eventually leapfrogging them by virtue of staying out longer for their sole refuelling stop. In the end, Trulli's dismal luck continued when his engine blew while in fifth place 11 laps from the end. That promoted Jenson to his place after which he received a

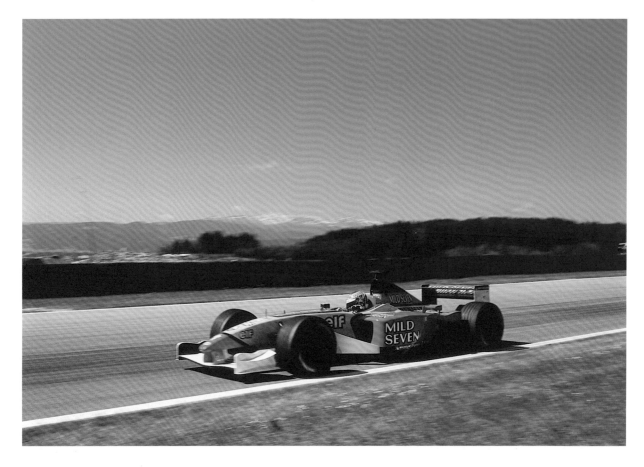

late race bonus when Raikkönen's right rear wheel hub failed four laps from the chequered flag and the Finn's McLaren pirouetted into retirement.

As he settled into his business class seat for the 14-hour flight back to Europe, Jenson could have been forgiven for permitting himself a wry grin. With three of the season's races completed he was holding fourth place in the Drivers' Championship, admittedly with a modest six points that looked pretty slim when compared with Michael Schumacher's 24. He consolidated his position in the rankings with a respectable fifth place in the San Marino GP at Imola. But at the Spanish Grand Prix an even more promising result was snatched away by hydraulic failure after he'd qualified sixth and run as high as third at one point.

At the Circuit de Catalunya, Button was driving superbly. On the face of it this was quite a turn around, with Coulthard chasing the Renault for all he was worth

Jenson finished seventh in the 2002 Austrian Grand Prix at the A1-Ring, trailing Coulthard's McLaren by just half a second when he crossed the finishing line. (LAT)

Jenson and Jarno exchange their overalls for dinner jackets and their Renault cockpits for the back seat of a limousine to attend a function at the 2002 Monaco Grand Prix. (LAT)

in the opening phase. He duly gained time on Button through the first spate of refuelling stops and eventually outbraked him neatly into the right-hander beyond the pits at the start of lap 34. Disappointingly, thereafter Jenson found the car getting progressively more difficult to drive and Trulli nipped past only a couple of laps later.

'The car wasn't fantastic at the beginning of the race with high-speed understeer and oversteer in the slower corners,' he said. 'We didn't manage to adjust the car to correct this during the pit stops and then I had an hydraulic problem. The steering got very heavy and it was as if somebody had switched the electrics off towards the end.' With Coulthard finishing third behind Schumacher's Ferrari and Montoya's Williams, Jenson now found himself demoted to fifth place in the points table.

Of course, in theatrical terms, Renault were bit-part players on the F1 scene and that reality was to be dramatically underlined in the Austrian Grand Prix. The race ended with Rubens Barrichello handing Michael Schumacher victory on the final corner, just as he'd

given second place to him behind David Coulthard's McLaren 12 months earlier. This heavy-handed performance from Ferrari hardly endeared the Prancing Horse to the army of race fans in the grandstands, nor indeed to the FIA, which called the team's management to account at the next meeting of the World Motorsport Council. None of this really concerned Jenson who finished a decent seventh, the only Renault to finish after Trulli succumbed to fuel pressure problems.

Jenson seemed to be getting on well in the Renault camp. But was he? By the time the teams rolled into Monte Carlo for their customary annual binge with the billionaire brigade, there were some pit lane observers who smelt trouble in the air. Rumour had it that John Byfield's preliminary talks about extending Jenson's contract with Renault had run up against something of a brick wall in the shape of Flavio Briatore. The enigmatic Italian entrepreneur's FBB management company had a stake in Trulli's future, but he was less interested in Button. That was largely because he'd taken the young Spanish driver Fernando Alonso under his commercial wing a couple of years earlier, helped place him at Minardi for 2001 and later signed him as Renault's test driver. Although Button never showed any indication that he was uneasy, it must have been unsettling to have Briatore's nominee effectively sizing up the cockpit of his car even before the 2002 season reached the halfway mark.

Alonso was clearly something of a prodigy. Winner of the Spa F3000 race in 2000 when he was 19 years old, he had driven the uncompetitive Minardi with flashes of genius the following year. Sitting in the Monaco media centre, my colleague Nigel Roebuck suddenly commented, 'Who the hell is *that*?' We looked up to see an in-car cockpit shot of somebody working away with lightning reactions and razor-sharp precision. It was Alonso on a qualifying lap. Now he was bounding around the pits in a Renault shirt, keeping a watchful eye on Button.

Jenson qualified an excellent eighth on his third Formula One outing at Monaco, one place behind his team-mate. But in the race everything went wrong. He crept slightly on the grid, anticipating the start by a fraction of a second, for which transgression he was awarded a drive-through penalty. Overtaking in contemporary F1 is difficult enough in normal circumstances, let alone trying to climb back through the field in Monte Carlo from a lowly position near the back of the pack. He survived until lap 52 when he got a little too ambitious trying to overtake Olivier Panis's BAR-Honda at Ste Devote and the two cars rattled into the barriers.

'I think I just got a little excited at the start,' said Jenson. 'After that I was a bit surprised to be penalised as well, but once I got the car into clear air it was working well. As for the accident, I could see that Panis was struggling with his rear tyres and tried to pass him at Ste Devote. He didn't see me and just took his normal line.'

In Canada Button's car overheated into retirement but at the European Grand Prix at the Nürburgring he came home a heartening fifth, although by then he was down in seventh place in the Drivers' Championship with 10 points; Michael Schumacher had 76. Two

The European Grand Prix at the Nürburgring saw another excellent performance from Button in 2002. He came home fifth, the last unlapped runner. (LAT)

weeks later he had an undistinguished run in the British Grand Prix from which he retired with a loose front wheel with six laps to go. Things were not looking too promising now.

Meanwhile, behind the scenes contractual negotiations were in full flow. Briatore had decided that Alonso would drive for Renault in 2003. The decision was confirmed on the Saturday afternoon at the French Grand Prix. Suddenly Jenson looked ever-so-slightly beleaguered, enveloped in a fog of media speculation. What would he do now? Go to Jaguar perhaps to replace Eddie Irvine? No, it would be the BAR-Honda squad. Even before the French Grand Prix had begun, the team's PR staff were passing round invitations to a press conference in London the day after the race. Jenson and David Richards had signed on the dotted line, guaranteeing Button a long-term contract with the team that the millionaire rallying entrepreneur was absolutely determined to transform into a winning proposition.

It still looked something of a risk, but Richards was supremely confident. 'When you build a block of flats, or an office, first you build a hole in the ground and you follow that with substantial foundations,' he said. 'It may take a year, perhaps longer, before it becomes obvious what you are doing, before the building rises above the ground, but all that time you are working away behind the scenes preparing for the future. That's what it was like at BAR during the summer of 2002. We knew where we intended to go, but it wasn't always easy to persuade people that we might get there in the end. But we were certainly working towards that aim.'

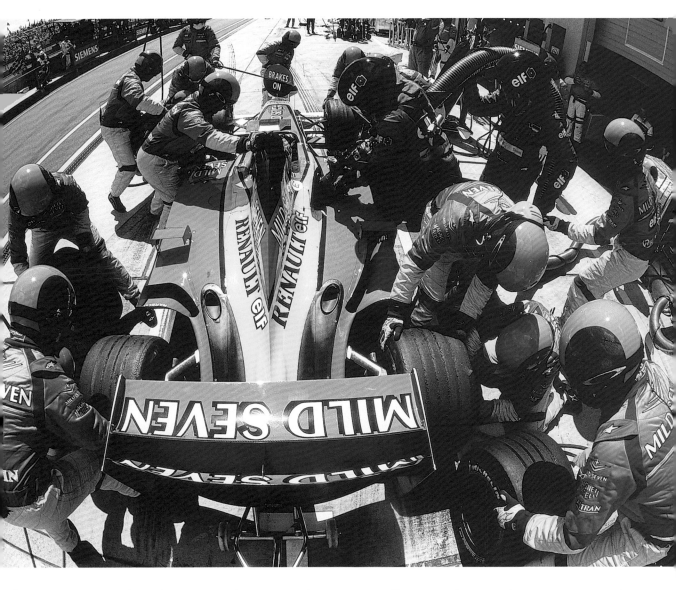

Button was to replace Olivier Panis in the BAR squad as the Frenchman had accepted an invitation to switch to the Toyota team. Olivier would be a hard act for Jenson to follow. Not only was he a highly popular, charismatic personality, but he'd arrived at BAR with a well merited reputation as a test and development driver. That reputation was built up with McLaren, where both David Coulthard and Mika Häkkinen had developed total faith in his conclusions about the cars he'd been driving. He was also very quick and his convivial nature ensured that he got on well with

Jacques Villeneuve, the sometimes temperamental former champion who was still very much a central character in the BAR-Honda story.

Villeneuve's response to the news of Button's impending arrival was so matter-of-fact as to border on the totally disinterested. 'I guess he will bring youth to the team,' he said dismissively. 'But not experience, as he hasn't got much. Last year [2001] was a season lost for him, but this year he has overshadowed Trulli and has been doing a good job. We get along. That is very important, because it is never enjoyable to be around someone you don't like.' On reflection, the implications of Villeneuve's comments were curious. Button was coming into the BAR-Honda squad with three years' experience as a grand prix driver under his belt. He was therefore hardly inexperienced. Yet perhaps Villeneuve was being very shrewd by not identifying Button as a serious rival. Perhaps he wanted to keep him guessing as to what his real feelings were. It was difficult to say, but then Jacques had always been a very difficult person to read.

The net result of all this activity was that Button entered that strange limbo land occupied by drivers who are seeing out their contract with one team in the knowledge that arrangements are already in place for them to move to another team the following year. No matter how hard you try to avoid the situation, there is inevitably a perceptible cooling of the relationship. So it was with Renault and Button. Their interest in him seemed to cool ever so slightly, fuelled in part by the fact that Alonso was already testing regularly for the team. In their mind he was the next Big Thing. Jenson was yesterday's news. Yet for all that, there remained a

Shaving the
barrier on his way
to sixth place in
the 2002 French
Grand Prix at
Magny-Cours, the
meeting at which
it was formally
announced that
Alonso would take
his place in the
team the next
season. (LAT)

certain respect for the young British driver and Mike Gascoyne later commented on several occasions that his personal biggest disappointment in 2002 was Button's failure to finish on the podium in Malaysia after such a superb drive.

Button finished sixth in the French Grand Prix, but when he arrived at Hockenheim, the newly truncated track near Heidelberg which played host to the German Grand Prix, he found himself battling against the tide. He lost half the Saturday free practice session due to an

engine failure, which effectively left him desperately attempting to regain lost ground. 'I then made a couple of mistakes on my qualifying run which meant that I couldn't improve on 13th,' he said. In the race he retired after 24 laps with transmission problems.

In Hungary Button spun off and in the Belgian Grand Prix at Spa-Francorchamps he suffered an engine failure ten laps into the 44-lap event. Things went better at Monza, although having to start in 17th place after a spin into a gravel trap didn't look too promising by the end of Saturday afternoon. Come the race, things proved much better. He and Trulli both did a great job, the two Renault drivers opting for one-stop refuelling strategies with a short opening stint, which carried them through to fourth and fifth places at the finish.

'I thought I'd lost everything at the start,' said Trulli. 'First gear didn't engage properly when I went through the launch control process, so I had to start from the back of the grid. After that, finishing fourth was pretty unexpected. Mika Salo's Toyota held us both up during the early stages of the race, so we decided to modify our strategy and make our pit stop earlier than planned.' At the flag, Jarno was just 6 seconds behind Eddie Irvine's Jaguar.

Just two races were left now in Jenson's Renault

All change! The
day after the
French Grand
Prix Jenson
attended a media
conference in
London with David
Richards where it
was announced
that he would
switch to the
BAR-Honda squad
in 2003. (LAT)

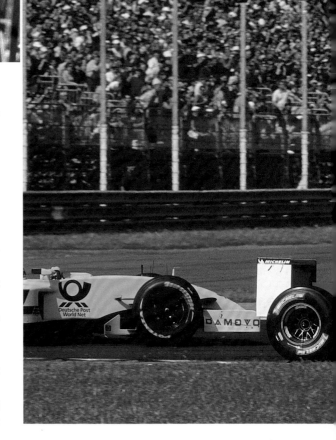

Jenson spins off during the 2002 Hungarian Grand Prix in Budapest, one of his rare disappointing performances of the season. (LAT)

career. He finished eighth in the US Grand Prix in Indianapolis and had a moderately satisfying finale at Suzuka where sixth in the Japanese race left him seventh in the championship on 14 points, one place ahead of team-mate Jarno Trulli on nine points. Michael Schumacher had more than ten times Jenson's tally, with 144 points to his credit.

At the end of the 2002 season Jenson rated ninth in the Top Ten driver ratings in the long-established *Autocourse* annual. They concluded, 'Button has proved himself a capable performer, yet there are still those who feel he is not sufficiently assertive when it comes to wheel-to-wheel scrapping. He is stylish and sympathetic with the machinery, shows a willingess to learn and is fundamentally very quick. Yet even though he is only 22, he has reached the end of his third season in Formula One without the benefit of the equipment needed to make a decisive mark on the record books. David Richards has said that he believes Button is capable of winning a world championship. This sounds

Seen here as the
meat in a very
tight Jordan
sandwich, Jenson
took the Renault
R202 to fifth
place behind Trulli
in the Italian
Grand Prix at
Monza. (LAT)

like a prediction made in the euphoria of the moment at the time he secured the services of the young British driver. Whether or not Button can deliver on Richards's promise will depend almost entirely on whether BAR can genuinely transform itself from a shambolic also-ran to the status of a genuine front-line contender.'

One thing seemed clear. For all his efforts to become part of the Renault family, Button seemed to have a slightly semi-detached relationship with Briatore's squad. Now at BAR he would find himself working for a team that wanted him unconditionally. The transformation would come. Not immediately. But things were set to get a lot better for Jenson Button's unfolding career prospects.

PRESS TO ACTIVATE

REFUEL

New team, new livery: Jenson is a BAR-Honda man at the start of 2003 (LAT)

squaring up to a champion

Relationships between team principals and their drivers are crucial to achieving grand prix success. While the driver will be looking for the ultimate performance, for all their outward toughness, the truth is that at this level they can display unexpected mental fragility. They need to get on with their employers and feel that those individuals are doing more than simply delivering their pay cheques.

You could see it in Nigel Mansell as he matured under the Williams team's tutelage in 1985. This wasn't a case of Williams producing a sympathetic arm around the shoulder. It was more a matter of giving him a positive environment in which he could unlock his talent. Button was the beneficiary of a similar set-up when he joined Williams in 2000. There was never any doubt in his mind that Frank and Patrick Head played straight with him. From the outset, he knew that Juan Pablo Montoya was lurking in the background as a likely successor in 2001. But Williams never made any secret of that obligation.

'Jenson will have to perform absolutely outstandingly if he is to keep Juan Pablo out of the team next season,' said Frank. So Button knew exactly where he was. The situation was less clear-cut during his time at Renault. The team principal Flavio Briatore was always a shrewd operator. When he took on Button in 2001 he seemed enthusiastic enough, outwardly at least. But paddock insiders never thought he displayed the burning confidence in the young British driver that was reflected by Frank and Patrick. He seemed a touch lukewarm.

From the start of 2002 it didn't look as though Button would have any long-term future at Renault, and so it proved. Briatore's protégé Fernando Alonso, a young Spaniard who had showed terrific natural car control in the tail-end Minardi the previous season, had been taken on to the Renault team as test driver.

The axe fell at the French Grand Prix. On the day before the race, Alonso was confirmed as Button's successor for 2003. Two days later BAR team principal David Richards moved quickly to reveal that he had signed Jenson on a four year contract, initially as Jacques Villeneuve's partner for the 2003 season. His salary would reputedly be around £3.5 million.

'I was staggered when I heard that Renault were releasing Jenson,' said Richards, 'and when I was made aware there was no binding issue between him and Williams, I immediately set about securing him. It happened quite quickly, but when you get an opportunity like this you don't sit on the sidelines. You make a quick decision. It's a two-year contract with a two-year option, but I look on it as a four-year contract as that's what it's going to be at the end of the day. And in that period I'm convinced that Jenson is going to be World Champion.'

For his part, Button was extremely grateful for the chance with BAR, even though there was the slim possibility that he might be tempted with a deal at Jaguar as Eddie Irvine was on schedule to leave at the end of the year if the team didn't renew his £5 million a year contract. Even so, Button was slightly taken aback when Briatore told him he would be out.

'Even though Renault was only an option,' he said, 'I was slightly shocked as it's been a good, positive season. I had a lot of teams I was talking to about where I wanted to go next year. I've been flattered by the enormous attention I've received as I've had a whole range of opportunities open to me. But one reason I've come here is because of David and what he has done with the team in the past six months. It's a team which will keep on improving.'

On the face of it this seemd like wild speculation, the sort of prediction made on the spur of the moment. But there was one key issue, absolutely fundamental to the whole package, on which any future success depended. As *Autocourse* noted at the end of 2002: 'Whether Button can deliver on Richards' promise will depend almost entirely on whether BAR can transform itself from a shambolic also-ran to the status of genuine front-line contender.'

Even in the summer of 2002, the BAR-Honda team was regarded as a bad joke in F1 circles. Conceived by Jacques Villeneuve's personal manager Craig Pollock as a vehicle to sustain the Canadian driver's career after he left Williams at the end of 1998, the project was bankrolled by the giant British American Tobacco concern. Here was a bunch of ambitious young entrepreneurs setting out to overturn the Formula One establishment. They were well-funded, they would operate from a new state-of-the-art factory at Brackley, near Silverstone, and they had the 1997 World Champion on their books as number one driver.

Yet as soon as the BAR-Supertec 001 rolled out onto the circuit at the 1999 Australian Grand Prix, dark clouds began to roll across Pollock's ambition. They finished the first season without scoring a single championship point. The car's performance had been inconsistent and unreliable. Even so, Honda came aboard in 2000 as their engine supply partner. But the only thing BAR proved itself good at was consuming money, oodles of it, an estimated £500 million in its first three years. By the

Strained relationship. Team-mates Jenson and Jacques Villeneuve at the official unveiling of the new BAR-Honda 005 in Barcelona. (LAT)

middle of 2001 Honda was at its wit's end with the team's management. They contacted BAT and made it quite clear that if a new regime was not put into place instead of Pollock, then they would be withdrawing from the partnership at the end of that season.

BAT agreed. The only other alternative was to cut their losses, scrap the whole programme and sell the team. That would have meant writing off what most people in the F1 paddock felt had been a singularly ill-judged investment in the first place.

BAT turned to David Richards to help dig them out of this pit of despair. They knew him well and trusted his judgement. Richards was steeped in motorsports know-how. He'd started out as a rally co-driver and won the 1981 World Rally Championship with Ari Vatanen in a semi-works Ford Escort. Then he'd retired and established his own specialist preparation company, eventually called 'Prodrive', which operated from a distinctive landmark base adjacent to the M40 motorway at Banbury. Prodrive's low, white-painted factory was as much its calling card as the company's expertise across the motorsports spectrum.

David's success and business skills led to a pivotal meeting with Fuji Heavy Industries at the Safari Rally in 1989, which would lead to the creation of the Subaru World Rally Team (SWRT) in a partnership which continues to thrive today.

Under David's direction the team embarked on a programme, initially in the British, and subsequently the Asia-Pacific and World Rally Championships (WRC). In 1990, it was David who spotted the raw talent of up-and-coming young driver Colin McRae and later Richard

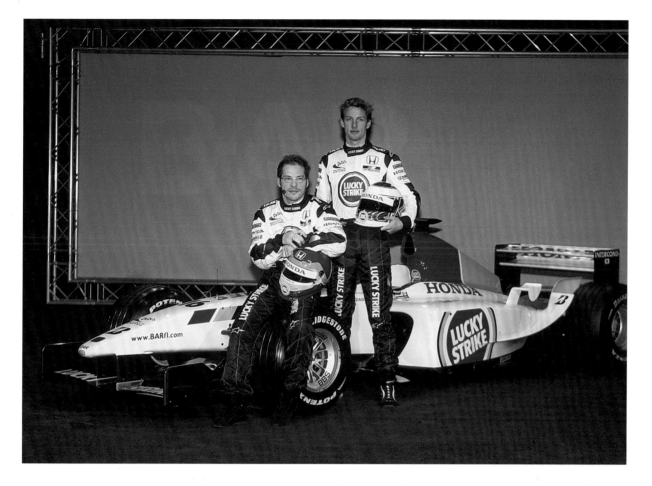

Burns. He personally oversaw the development of their early careers, leading to two British titles for Subaru and McRae in 1991 and 1992, and a further title for Burns in 1993. Through the 1990s, Prodrive turned the Subaru into the icon of world rallying with its familiar blue and yellow livery. It was this success in rallying that is credited with helping to turn around the fortunes of the Japanese company. And the whole programme has been sponsored for more than a decade by BAT's 555 cigarette brand.

Richards also had contemporary F1 experience. In 1998 he was approached by the Benetton family to help turn around the fortunes of its team, which was at that point making heavy weather of its mid-grid status. It had been a long-time ambition of Richards to get into Formula One and he seized the opportunity. But after a year of mixed fortunes, David found that he was not

given the opportunity to run the business in the way he wanted and returned to focus his attentions on expanding Prodrive at the end of the season. Benetton simply wanted a safe pair of hands to steer their operation. They weren't interested in the newcomer's views on strengthening the team's brand image or developing the driver line-up.

So it was hardly surprising that Richards thought twice when the mandarins at British American Tobacco approached him with the suggestion that he take over responsibility for the BAR-Honda squad. But, after some soul searching, he eventually agreed to take the job. But only on his terms.

'BAT, which was both part owner and sponsor of the team, approached me and asked me if I could come and help with this programme,' said Richards. 'So we went and talked about it at some length. I knew the people very well and could speak my mind. Can you take it over and run it for us? I told them I wasn't really minded to do this, but would write thoughts down on one sheet of A4 paper and if we could agree something on those terms, then we could do it.

'I wanted the authority to get on with the job, really to do it the way I wanted to do it. I was very concerned by the fact that they had minority shareholders in there and a rather complicated situation. I didn't want to go in and rattle a few cages only to be thrown out after a short time. We needed the security, and finally agreed a five-year term.

'When we arrived we found a team which clearly had the right resources and all the finances, but had still grossly underachieved,' he said. 'In the main there was a lack of leadership and no clear vision of how to achieve their aims. There is a peculiar viewpoint in F1 that the more money and the more people you have will make your car go quicker. You have to know how to spend it to best effect.'

Slipping into the BAR driving seat, Richards found that he had inherited Geoff Willis, the former Williams aerodynamicist, as the team's technical director – one of Pollock's more inspired recruits. Anxious to get costs under control, the new regime slashed the workforce from 450 to just under 400. It was certainly a start, but like a fully laden oil tanker attempting to change course, the delay between pushing the rudder controls and feeling the ship respond can be agonising. Willis joined BAR early during the 2002 season, but effectively inherited the team's 004 design from Malcolm Oastler. Not until 2003 could he replace what he described as a 'clunky, out-of-date, expensive to manufacture machine'. At the launch of the BAR 005 in January 2003, he commented, 'You have to start in a new ballpark and that's what we have done now.'

Yet there was a hidden, nagging sub-text to Richards' position. How did he rationalise his relationship with Pollock and Villeneuve? Ideally, his end game was to dispense with the team's founder as, logically, he felt that having the old management team still hanging around the team's motorhome was not a satisfactory situation. Yet the structure of the BAR shareholdings was complex and intricate, so it would be 2003 before

Pollock began to fade into the background and his presence in the paddock began to wane.

Yet Villeneuve started 2003 on a distinctly hostile note as far as Button was concerned. It was clear from his body language at the official launch of the BAR 005 that he didn't have much time for Button, believing his reputation to have been over-blown by the British media and emphasising that the Englishman still had to prove himself. He obliquely denigrated Jenson by references to his outgoing team-mate Olivier Panis who was switching to the fledgling Toyota squad.

'The key is whether you respect your team-mate or not,' said Villeneuve. 'If you do, as I did with Olivier, then everything is fine and nobody gets upset, but if you don't, then that can make things unhappy. He [Button] comes into the team seen as a future World Champion and I guess there's a lot of weight on his shoulders. I've won a World Championship in the past and people know what I can do. I believe it is important to be strong. You can't burst into tears if something goes wrong. That's one thing that I have a hard time to respect. Human strength is probably more important for respect than sheer speed.'

In retrospect, it is difficult to see what point Villeneuve was trying to get across. Button certainly did not have a reputation as an F1 cry-baby and it looked as though the Canadian was the one who was feeling the pressure. For the first time in his BAR career he was squaring up to a team-mate who hadn't been recruited by Craig Pollock. Perhaps inwardly he knew that Richards was preparing to put his own personal form under intense scrutiny. The new team principal had inherited Villeneuve's water-tight $18 million contract for 2003 and it was clear that he regarded the Canadian – indeed any driver with such a price tag – as a luxury BAR could well do without.

Button, who was earning barely one-third of his team-mate's fee, reacted coolly to Villeneuve's thinly veiled critique. He made it crystal clear that he wasn't about to be intimidated. 'The press always likes to build up tension when a new driver joins a team, but I think we can work together,' he said. 'When you have the possibilities of winning you can fight each other, but we really have to work together to move this team forward

Thinking about the future. Jenson in the pit lane in Barcelona prior to pre-season testing with the BAR-Honda 005, 15 January 2003. (LAT)

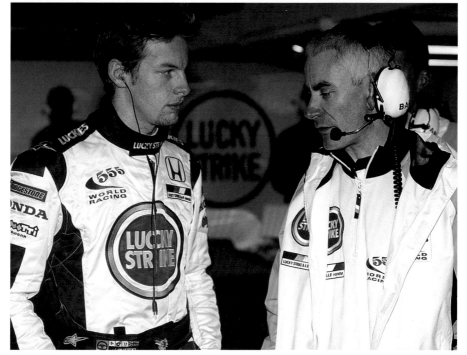

Button talks technical with Geoff Willis, the former Williams aerodynamicist who became BAR's technical director at the end of 2001. (LAT)

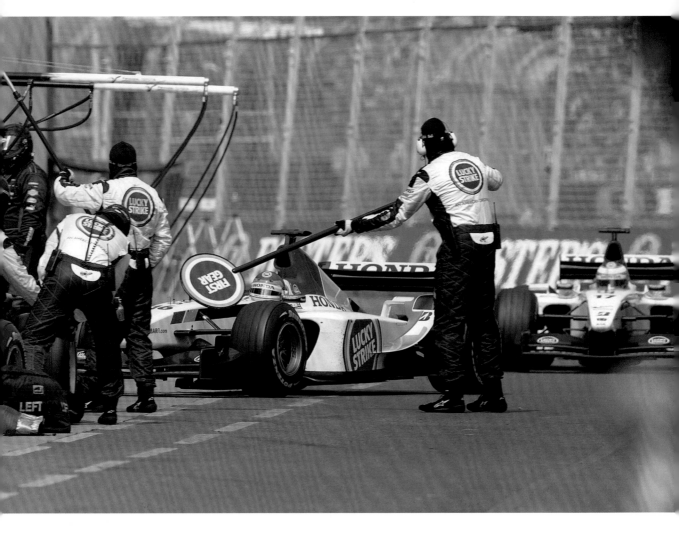

and I am sure we can do that. I have had difficult team-mates in the past. Ralf Schumacher was tough to begin with, Jarno Trulli could be a bit hard, so that doesn't really bother me.'

Pre-season testing was inconclusive. The new car was certainly a significant improvement over its predecessor, but Honda clearly needed to raise its game and had taken steps to do so. They ran an all-new V10 for the first time on the dyno in the summer of 2002. The engine initially looked very promising, but the development programme suffered a setback in the first race of the 2003 season in Melbourne after a problem with a batch of camshafts.

There was also an all-new Honda engine which first

Jenson's debut race for BAR in Melbourne was fraught with tension after it seemed as though Villeneuve had deliberately pitted for fuel on the same lap as he was scheduled to come in. (Sutton Images)

Button eventually finished tenth in Australia, one place behind his team-mate. (LAT) ran on the dyno in August 2002 and ran in a car right from the first Barcelona winter test. The policy was to upgrade it throughout the off-season, with a further five upgrades in power (giving between 0.3 and 2.0 per cent) and a reduction in weight totalling between 5 and 10 per cent over the year. In fact, they went back a step in Melbourne with the camshaft problem, but that was corrected by Malaysia.

Thus armed, Button and Villeneuve prepared to do battle in Melbourne, the first race of 2003 marked by the introduction of a new one-by-one, Indy-style qualifying format. The running order of the Friday session was reversed for the crucial Saturday session, which would determine the grid positions. That second

session on Saturday saw Jacques exerting the upper hand, the Canadian qualifying sixth on 1m 28.420s, just 0.2s ahead of Jenson.

'It's difficult to know where we stand compared with everybody else, but I'm pretty happy with eighth position,' he reflected. 'It's a good place to be starting the first race of the season. It wasn't a particularly great lap and like everybody else, there was room for improvement. We're starting from a points' scoring position, though, so I'm still feeling confident for the race.'

The Ferrari F2002s of Michael Schumacher and Rubens Barrichello had buttoned up the front row of the grid, as expected, and surged away into immediate

1–2 formation, despite the initially patchy damp track conditions. But Jenson made a great start in the BAR and came round in sixth place, just ahead of Jacques, at the end of a satisfying opening lap.

The seamless Maranello machine may have looked on course for another dominant performance, but the reality of the situation was rather different. Barrichello was struggling with discomfort from his 'HANS' head and neck restraint system and spun off into the wall on lap six. The safety car was deployed to slow the pack while the debris was cleared and the track swept clean at the accident sight. On lap 12 the race proper restarted, but only four laps later Mark Webber's Jaguar lurched to a stop out on the circuit with a rear suspension problem. The car was judged to have come to rest at a potentially vulnerable spot, so the safety car was deployed for the second time.

The race was restarted again on lap 21 with Kimi Raikkonen's McLaren now leading Michael Schumacher, who was followed by David Coulthard's McLaren and the BAR-Hondas of Villeneuve and Button. At the end of lap 25 both BARs headed for the pit lane, a furious Button being subjected to a time-consuming delay as he queued up behind his team-mate.

'I had radio problems, so it was very difficult to communicate with the pit wall and both cars ended up pitting at the same time,' said Villeneuve. 'It took a long time to get the tyres working and I didn't get enough time on any set.'

Button, who clearly suspected that Villeneuve had deliberately come into the pits in a bid to spoil his efforts, was certainly not amused. 'Jacques did not come in when he was supposed to,' he said. 'I was a little bit shocked when he came in because I knew I was on the right lap. He did apologise, which was needed, I think. But I am not very impressed. It is very annoying. It was a bit of a nightmare for everyone.'

Frustrating it may have been, but this was also an instructive psychological lesson for Button. In a peculiar way, Villeneuve had shown his hand. After adopting such a chippy, almost dismissively aggressive, attitude towards Jenson in the run-up to the season, one could almost discern that Jacques was now slightly on the back foot. If he was to have a future in a post-Pollock BAR

Button chats with David Richards during the 2003 Australian Grand Prix weekend. The two men quickly established a good relationship. (LAT)

squad, he would have to perform against this youthful incomer, almost ten years his junior. Suddenly that $18 million retainer looked less like an acknowledgement of Jacques's status as the 1997 World Champion, and more like an albatross of expectancy hanging heavily around his neck. Even at this early stage, Jenson seemed to be gaining the upper hand.

When he arrived in Kuala Lumpur ten days later to start preparations for the Malaysian Grand Prix, Button adopted a slightly amused and ironic tone as he reflected on the mishap in Melbourne.

'Yeah, the radios are fixed now, they work now,' he grinned. 'Mine's fine. After the race a lot of work has gone into making sure the radios are working well. Hopefully they will be good here. I feel I've settled into BAR very well and I feel very happy. The most comfortable I think I've been in Formula One and probably the team that I've been most happy with. Everyone seems very positive and we're all working together very, very well. They have also listened to what I say from the word go, which has been very important.'

On a slightly crisper note he later added, 'To see a definite points finish, a very possible top-six place dashed because your team-mate decides to come in and refuel on the same lap that [you] had been told to, is, to put it lightly, frustrating. His explanation afterwards was that he had a problem with his radio at the precise time when I was coming in. He had no further problems afterwards.'

Jenson also reflected on the fact that Sepang had been the scene of one of his best-ever races in the Renault 12 months earlier and he had high hopes for another strong performance in the new BAR. 'I'm in it to win,' he said firmly, 'and finally I believe I am in a car that should consistently score points, might make a few podiums and could deliver my maiden victory. That's why I can't wait for this weekend in Kuala Lumpur. Just as long as my team-mate doesn't hold me up again!'

In the event the Malaysian race delivered rather less than was hoped for the two BAR-Honda drivers. Jenson at least had the satisfaction off qualifying ninth, three places ahead of Villeneuve, but the former World Champion didn't even make it to the start. Just before his car left the garage prior to the final parade lap, it developed an electrical problem. Then, at the start of the parade lap, the problem returned and damaged the gearbox. It seems that the main vehicle computer reset itself due a sudden voltage 'spike' through the system. That effectively scrambled the car's gear selection capability – the transmission attempted to select two gears at once and damaged the selectors.

There was a cruel helping of late race disappointment for Jenson as he dropped from fifth to seventh on the final lap behind Michael Schumacher's Ferrari and Jarno Trulli's Renault. 'It was a very tiring race and the car was so difficult to drive,' said Button. 'I had very low grip and the oversteer got progressively worse towards the end. It destroyed the rear tyres. I held off Jarno for as long as I could, then on the last corner I braked where I normally would and the rear just locked up. I went straight on and Michael was able to get through.'

Nevertheless, seventh place was a success of sorts. Included in the revised rule package for 2003 was a new points scoring system which rewarded the top eight finishers rather than the top six. So Jenson came away from Malaysia with two championship points, BAR's first of the new season. Villeneuve had yet to score.

Jacques rectified that situation a fortnight later when he dodged every hazard to finish sixth in the Brazilian Grand Prix at Sao Paolo's spectacular – and on this

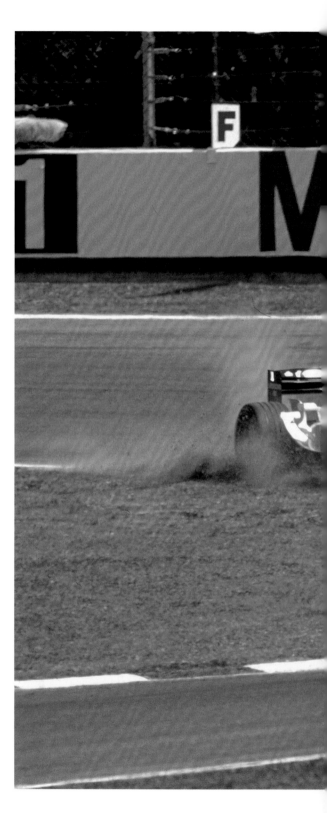

Embarrassing
moment! Jenson
accidentally
pushes his pal
David Couthard's
McLaren off the
road as he makes
to overtake in the
2003 Spanish
Grand Prix. (LAT)

occasion, near flooded – Interlagos circuit. Even Michael Schumacher was caught out by the impossible conditions, but the fact that the world's greatest F1 driver of his generation made a slip was no consolation for Jenson who slammed off the road quite heavily.

The race was won by Jordan's Giancarlo Fisichella – one of Jenson's former team-mates – in circumstances so convoluted and bizarre that the Italian driver had to wait five days before the success was confirmed. It was ten days before he eventually got his hands on the winner's trophy.

Fisichella was propelled into the limelight when Mark Webber, struggling for grip on worn Michelin rubber, crashed spectacularly coming through the fast left-hand kink before the pit. Webber's car ended up alongside the barrier on the left of the track, its driver shaken but unhurt, but debris was scattered all across the circuit.

As the dust settled, Fisichella ducked through the debris, but then Fernando Alonso – Button's successor in the Renault squad – arrived at speed over the crest and slammed straight into one of the Jaguar's wheels, which was lying in the middle of the circuit. That in turn slammed the young Spanish driver sharp right into the retaining wall. Both impacts were in excess of 30G and it said much for the standards of contemporary F1 car construction that Alonso escaped with nothing more serious than bruised legs. He was taken to hospital for a precautionary check-up.

The onset of heavy rain on race morning posed a serious potential problem for the Michelin runners, including McLaren, Williams and Jaguar. Their choice of designated race tyre was closer to a deep grooved full

wet tyre than the relatively lightly grooved intermediate, which was available to the Bridgestone runners.

The FIA officials announced at 12.30pm, with almost painful formality, that a 'change in climatic conditions had occurred'. In other words it was now tipping it down, so teams were allowed to change various chassis settings and switch to rain tyres.

This edict notwithstanding, for a time it really looked as if the Brazilian GP might not take place at all. The cars were lined up on the starting grid, but the conditions seemed too risky to take the gamble. Eventually it was decided that the race would start 15 minutes late and that it would be run behind the safety car for the first few laps.

For nine laps the pack circulated steadily behind the safety car, then Bernd Maylander aimed the silver Mercedes CLK coupé for the sanctuary of the pit lane and the pack was unleashed with David Coulthard surging through to take the lead from Barrichello going into the first corner after the pits.

Going into lap 18, Ralph Firman's Jordan suffered a right front suspension breakage approaching the braking area for the left-hander after the pits at around 175mph. The errant wheel folded up onto the nose section of the yellow car and Firman became a passenger as it tobogganed into the back of Olivier Panis's Toyota TF103, eliminating both cars from the race. With debris all over the track, the safety car was deployed for the second time that afternoon.

Raikkonen stayed out behind the safety car, but the next ten cars all came in for top-ups while the pack was still running at reduced speed. At the start of lap 23 the field was again unleashed with Raikkonen completing that lap 1.7s ahead of Coulthard with Michael Schumacher third ahead of Cristiano da Matta's Toyota, which had yet to stop, and Barrichello.

Even though the track surface was getting progressively drier by this point, rivulets of water were coursing across the circuit at turn three. On lap 25 Montoya became the first casualty of this slippery section, slamming off the road into the barrier. His Williams was soon followed by Antonio Pizzonia, then Michael Schumacher, on lap 27, also spun off the road, triggering the third safety car spell of the race.

Jenson crosses the line to take a strong fourth place in the 2003 Austrian Grand Prix, one of the early signs that things were looking up for the BAR-Honda squad. (LAT)

On lap 30 the race restarted yet again, but only three laps later Button slammed off the road at turn three in what was a very heavy impact. 'I just caught the standing water a little too much,' said Jenson. 'I tried to save it, but that just sent me into the tyre wall. I went in quite heavily and my back is aching a little, but it could have been much worse. It's disappointing, but that's the way it goes.'

There was nothing more for Jenson to do than change out of his sodden overalls, nip back to the hotel for a quick shower and take a cab out to Sao Paolo's Guarulhos international airport for the long flight back to London. Two weeks ahead lay the San Marino Grand Prix at Imola and the start of the intensive European leg of the World Championship.

The BAR-Honda 005s performed well in qualifying at the evocatively named Autodromo Enzo e Dino Ferrari. Jacques lined up seventh, two places ahead of Jenson. 'The first two sectors of my qualifying lap were okay,' shrugged Button by way of explanation. 'But then I went a little wide at the high-speed chicane up the hill and lost a bit of time. I also had a bit too much understeer on the high-speed corners.'

This was a particularly emotional weekend for Jenson's former team-mate at Williams, Ralf Schumacher, and his brother Michael. They started preparations for the race knowing that their mother Elisabeth was critically ill at a hospital in Germany; the boys flew back in Michael's private jet to see her on Saturday evening. Sadly, she died that same night, ensuring that Michael's victory celebrations would be sober and muted when he scored

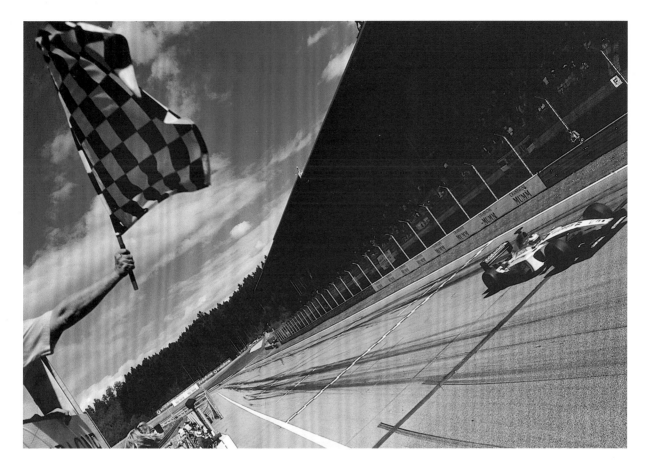

his latest F1 victory the following afternoon. It was one of those personal tragedies that tend to put everything else into sharp perspective.

The Spanish Grand Prix at Barcelona's Circuit de Catalunya could also have been a good one. Jenson qualified fifth but there were five cars in front of him after his pit stop, so he felt he had to try to pass them. Audaciously, perhaps, he went down the inside of David Coulthard going into the 18th lap and he turned in. Button damaged the car and had to come in for a new nose. He finished ninth, two laps behind Michael Schumacher's winning Ferrari F2003. But Coulthard remained beached in the gravel and had to retire.

'In such circumstances it's perhaps inevitable that you both think you're in the right, so then you look at the video tape and say it's just a racing incident,' said Jenson. 'I mean we're good friends, so immediately after the race I went to his motorhome and we sat and watched it. We needed to sort it out, because we were flying back to Monaco immediately after the race – in his plane!'

The two British drivers duly shook hands and made up. Two weeks later, in what would turn out to be the last Austrian Grand Prix at the A1-Ring, Button finished fourth ahead of Coulthard. It equalled Jenson's career best result so far. 'I had a great race today; I really enjoyed it,' he said. 'This is what the team really needed and deserved, but it wasn't a fluke. We really deserved our result today.'

Finally, on the eve of the first practice session for the Monaco Grand Prix, Button revealed that his feud with Jacques Villeneuve was finally over. The two men had been at loggerheads even before the start of the season after Villeneuve had insisted that Button had yet to prove his reputation on the track, then likened the 23-year-old Brit to a member of a boy band.

105

Marshals work carefully to extricate Jenson from his badly damaged BAR-Honda after his crash in practice at Monaco in 2003. (LAT)

Button admitted that they had buried the hatchet and were collaborating to develop the new BAR-Honda 005. 'I think we both said a few things that were a little bit pathetic,' said Jenson. 'But they had to be said. The thing is we are both very competitive. But we are working pretty well together now, which is good.' David Richards added, 'There was a little bit of friction between him and Jacques earlier on which we have managed to control now and point in the right direction.'

That view was endorsed by Geoff Willis, the BAR technical director who worked with both drivers at Williams, albeit at separate times. 'I am impressed at just how much both drivers have developed since I last worked with them,' he said. 'Jacques was always one tough cookie, but he is technically much better than he was at Williams. Certainly he is very sensitive – and better in the wet – and has clearly spent a lot of time thinking through his approach.'

As far as Button is concerned, Willis said that he never had to be told twice about any technical aspect of the car during his debut F1 season in 2000. 'Not only do I think he is faster than he was then, but now he's got such a library of experience to draw upon that he's turned into much more of a thinking driver,' he said. 'Interestingly, while Jenson has certainly got the knack of this new one-lap qualifying format – pushing to the edge without making a mistake – Jacques is perhaps a little better at race set-up. But they are very well matched.'

Yet hardly had this personal harmony been restored within the team than Button found himself out of the Monaco Grand Prix in an abrupt and fearful manner.

During the second practice session on Thursday

morning, he lost control of his car coming out of the tunnel. It slammed sideways into a protective barrier at the end of the chicane escape road. The crash was a carbon-copy of Karl Wendlinger's terrifying crash in practice for the 1994 race, which resulted in the German driver being hospitalised and left in a coma for over a fortnight. Eventually Wendlinger made a recovery and raced again, but he never regained his F1 form and soon dropped from the senior formula to finish his career driving sports and touring cars.

Thankfully, the huge improvements in lateral cockpit protection – notably the high sided support structures now demanded as part of the F1 design process – meant that Button escaped with little more than concussion and a severe shaking. He also benefited from the latest seat technology available to F1 drivers, which means the seat can be removed from the cockpit in the event of an accident without having to remove the driver first.

A decade before the low cockpit sides of Wendlinger's Sauber made him painfully vulnerable in a high-impact lateral accident and he had to be lifted from the car and placed on a stretcher on the ground before the medical crew could work on him.

Button was taken to hospital where he remained overnight as a precaution. There was even talk that he might take part in the race, starting from the pit lane. In the event, wisely, he gave it a miss.

'I've never really had a big accident in F1 but it doesn't scare me at all,' he said. 'You never know if it will but it didn't scare me at all in this one. I'm looking forward to getting back in the car but I also don't want to be silly about it. I want to go through all the training regime first and make sure everything's good. I don't want to get back into the car and hurt myself. We have to make sure everything's okay before I do that.'

Button admitted he'd been pushing too hard. 'What makes it so frustrating is that it was a bloody good lap,' he told his father John when he visited his bedside later in the day. It certainly was a huge shame, as Jenson had been third fastest behind the two Ferraris during Thursday's first qualifying session and looked a strong contender on his fourth outing at Monaco.

'After I hit the wall I was unconscious. I don't know for

Jenson could be a good sport. In the summer of 2003 he drove the author round Silverstone in this London taxicab as part of a feature previewing the British Grand Prix for *F1 Racing* magazine. (LAT)

how long. I sort of came round and they [the rescue team] had already cut [through the seat] up to my arm. I might have been awake but I can't really remember,' he recalled. 'I was speaking to [FIA medical head] Sid Watkins and he was saying that I was talking but I wasn't making any sense,' said Button. 'I said what's different? I mean, that's me all over. I didn't have a clue where I was. I was just looking down and my legs were hurting.'

This unfortunate episode left Jenson ticking off the days until the Thursday morning before the Montreal race to hear whether he would be given the medical all-clear to compete in the Canadian Grand Prix. After the crash at Monaco, he had hoped to return to the cockpit for the following week's test at Monza. But he was examined by FIA medical delegate Prof. Sid Watkins earlier in the week and, on his advice, Button was persuaded to wait until Canada before trying to drive again.

'There was still some interruption to his memory when I saw him on the Tuesday after Monaco,' said Watkins. 'We are particularly mindful of the consequences of what we call the "second impact" syndrome – where a driver suffers a second concussion a short time after the first impact.' Under FIA regulations, the licence of any F1 driver who is hospitalised after an accident is automatically suspended until he his 're-integrated' after another medical inspection. In this case Button had to be examined by Watkins and the Montreal circuit's chief medical officer Jacques Bouchard.

Amazingly, Button's crashed car had already been totally repaired and Jenson was scheduled to race it in Montreal. 'The structural integrity of the modern F1 car is quite remarkable, a testimony to the engineering of the teams and the safety rules promoted by the FIA,' said BAR team principal David Richards.

In stark contrast, the structure of some personal relationships within the BAR team were beginning to look beyond repair. Eddie Irvine, the former Jaguar F1 driver, knew both Villeneuve and Button well and offered the view that the situation had become too complicated.

'I think this year Jenson's made a lot of mistakes and still has long way to go,' Irvine said at Montreal. 'But I have to say he's also made a lot of progress, is coming on well and has certainly been faster than I expected. On the face of it, Jenson has been blowing Jacques away, but you've got to ask yourself why. Well, Jenson has certainly grown mentally, but the fact remains that [Giancarlo] Fisichella had the extra pace to beat him at Renault last year. So has he suddenly got better, or has the environment Villeneuve finds himself in this year worked against him?

'To be honest, I think it's a bit of both. It's no secret that Jacques has problems with the team and it's certainly hurting him. He's upset with the way things have been handled and now he's got a situation where Jenson looks like a hero and he's got a team boss [David Richards] who doesn't want him in the car.'

Richards' irritation over Villeneuve's $18 million contract for 2003 intensified as the season wore on. Put simply, he thought the money could be spent to better effect elsewhere. In a bid to re-direct these crucial funds to the task of developing the car, he had earlier attempted to broker a deal which would have seen Villeneuve drive in the US-based CART series in 2003

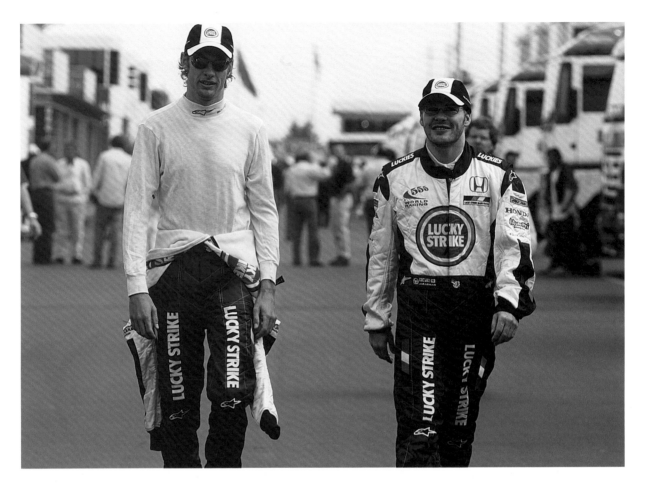

before returning to BAR to see out the extra year of his deal in 2004. But this plan never reached fruition and Richards continued to make little secret of his frustration at having to pay so much for a driver who was not his first choice.

Richards did try to be conciliatory and positive towards Villeneuve in the run-up to the Canadian race, claiming that he had the ability to regain the form which carried him to the 1997 World Championship at the wheel of a Williams-Renault.

'For Jacques, it is psychological,' said Richards. 'It's been a tough start to the season for him with the number of retirements he's had. He knows he is still competitive and he knows that he has a competitive car. If it clicks at the right time, he will re-emerge as a real force to be reckoned with.' But Villeneuve was above all else a realist. He acknowledged that he might have to accept a

deal from a lesser team if an offer to renew was not forthcoming from BAR-Honda at the end of the season.

Whatever happened, Villeneuve faced a significant drop in salary from his current position as the second highest earner in F1 after Michael Schumacher. But he also had a reputation for being an independent free spirit who sought to limit his personal appearances and autograph signing sessions for the fans, something which could work against him in the future. He remained sanguine about that reality.

'The teams will do everything they can to bring down your value and your management will do everything they can to up it,' he said. 'That's just the market.' The market in the middle of 2003 was certainly moving in Jenson Button's direction as far as consolidating the Englishman's status as an emerging star was concerned. He was asserting his edge over Villeneuve.

All friends now. Jenson and Jacques Villeneuve walk the paddock at Nürburgring during the European Grand Prix weekend, their earlier disagreements now apparently behind them. (LAT)

Jenson and his girlfriend, Louise Griffiths. He has said on many occasions that she is the rock on which he relies. (LAT)

But the BAR-Honda package was generally neither quick enough nor sufficiently reliable through the summer of 2003. Neither car finished in Canada. Then Jenson comprehensively outclassed Jacques in the European Grand Prix before the Canadian retired with transmission trouble. But in the French Grand Prix he had to park his car out on the circuit, its tank run dry, after a problem with the team's refuelling rig meant that not enough fuel went in at a scheduled stop.

At Silverstone there was more disappointment. He qualified 20th, and last, after he clipped a kerb at Becketts and broke a front suspension push-rod. Under the circumstances, his climb back to eighth place was quite an impressive performance. That was followed by

Jenson and Louise prior to the impromptu lawnmower race at the 2003 British Grand Prix. (LAT)

Monitoring the opposition. Button and Richards in the BAR-Honda garage at the 2003 British Grand Prix. (LAT)

Great day. Jenson forced the BAR-Honda into the lead of the 2003 US Grand Prix at Indianapolis, but its engine expired in the closing stages. (LAT) another eighth at Hockenheim, tenth in Hungary and retirement with a gearbox problem at Monza. But then came the US Grand Prix at Indianapolis and Jenson, although he failed to finish, was at least left with a broad grin on his face.

Button finished the season on a high note. He led at Indianapolis and again at Suzuka, where he finished fourth. Earlier in the year he'd run strongly to finish fourth in Austria and repeated that in Japan, two places ahead of Takuma Sato, who replaced Villeneuve as his team-mate with one race of the season still to run. Yet it was the US GP that gave him the sense of anticipation that his long overdue place on the podium, his first top three finish, was at last within his reach.

'To be leading for 15 laps at Indianapolis was an amazing feeling,' he smiled reflectively. 'Okay, to be in

that position we were really a bit lucky. We judged it correctly, switching to wet tyres when the rain was falling. Even though we weren't going to win, we still had a good chance of finishing second to Michael, although I think Kimi [Raikkonen] would have been quite close.

'In the wet we were pretty strong. I'd already gone through . . . , you know, when you have tread on the rear wet tyres it's a big problem when the track is drying. I'd already gone through that process, but looking at Michael's tyres he still had to go through that. But I think I could have stayed pretty close to him in the wet. In the dry it would have been a different thing, but I think we would have been finishing second.'

Ironically, despite the initial tension of their relationship, Jenson obviously felt quite reflective about

Jacques when he realised at Suzuka that he was gone from the BAR-Honda equation, replaced by Sato. 'It was strange once he had gone,' he said. 'Quite strange. And I found myself missing him really. It took me a little time, but I eventually realised that he is quite a fun guy. Very opinionated, but quite funny at times. But I always suspected it might be a problem coming into the team at the start of the season, because there was quite a lot of press about me moving to the team and I knew that Jacques wouldn't like that.'

So the 2003 season ended on a high note for Button, although the overall paucity of hard results inevitably looked as though it might lead him into that curious limbo land which bridges the gulf between a driver perceived as a bright young star and an established old

Best drive of his year. Jenson also briefly led at Suzuka, but stormed home a strong fourth in his new role as *de facto* BAR-Honda team leader. (LAT)

hand. He developed a good relationship with BAR team principal David Richards who continued to insist that he was World Championship potential. The ease and assurance which Jenson radiated as he led those laps at Indianapolis served as a flickering reminder of what he might achieve given the right equipment.

Yet there was still that nagging question to be answered. Was Jenson Button really good enough to get the job done at the highest level?

Button with new
team-mate
Takuma 'Darcy'
Sato during tests
in Barcelona,
November 2003.
(LAT)

Jenson with
Louise on the
evening they
attended the
2003 *Autosport*
Awards. (LAT)

Golden moment. Jenson leads World Champion Michael Schumacher's Ferrari at Imola, 2004. (LAT)

aiming for the big time

Sir Jackie Stewart arrived in the paddock at Silverstone, three days prior to the 2004 British Grand Prix, in suitable style. Immaculately dressed, as always, he climbed from a black chauffeur-driven Jaguar limousine and briefly reflected that no fewer than 39 years had passed since he scored his own first Formula One victory, driving a BRM in the non-championship International Trophy race. In the process, he beat reigning World Champion John Surtees, in a Ferrari, into second place.

The question begging to be asked, even before Sir Jackie could don his carefully pressed tartan sports jacket, was could Button do the same in this year's British Grand Prix. Could he take the fight to another World Champion in a Ferrari, the great Michael Schumacher? Stewart weighed his words carefully, but his answer left no doubt that he was a huge fan of the young British driver.

'Jenson has all the qualities that make a grand prix winner and his time is sure to come,' he replied. 'Even if the challenge of getting on terms with Michael Schumacher's Ferrari may be too much for him to claim victory in front of what is expected to be a capacity 100,000-strong home crowd cheering him on at Silverstone tomorrow.'

He also insisted that Button's status in the Formula One business had been enhanced by the fact that he overcame a serious streak of immaturity during his debut season with Williams in 2000 and that he was now one of the most rounded performers on the starting grid. 'I think Jenson has surprised quite a few perceptive people in the business,' he continued, 'and by that I'm thinking of people like Bernie Ecclestone and perhaps even myself who felt that he progressed a little too far too soon.

'When Jenson got to the Formula 3 level, for whatever reason, I think he got a bit carried away with the rate of his progress. We met him and his people at that time when we were running [our own team] Paul Stewart Racing, but there were far too high expectations from all concerned at that time. There was no doubt that they saw in him something special, but the manner in which it was dealt with by his people, and even himself, suggested to me that it could possibly end in tears.

'His personal disciplines and manner of dealing with life showed a degree of immaturity, which I feared might not be removed as he developed. Having seen that at functions, and other activities, I feared he might not make the grade because of his mind not recognising the disciplines required to achieve in the big time.

'He has done a remarkable job in that respect, and that is probably the single most important element that has positioned him in what I think today has made him a potential winner of every grand prix this season. He drives well, he thinks well, he presents himself well, he behaves well and it's important for him that he retains those qualities. I think he had started that process before David Richards [the BAR team principal] came

117

along, but David has unquestionably added to it and confirmed in Jenson's mind what he needs to do to make the big time.'

Yet Stewart also emphasised what a difficult psychological barrier it can be breaking through to win your first Formula One race. 'The great thing you can say of every young driver is that he's got potential,' he said. 'But ultimately you have to translate that into winning . . .'

'It happened to me when I started in Formula One, but I had the benefit of knowing the disciplines I had to live with in order to be competitive in my shooting career before I ever started motor racing. Jenson didn't have that benefit, and it showed. But what he's done is collect himself very well and if he retains that focus, commitment and discipline, I think he has a tremendous future ahead of him.'

Crucially, by the start of the 2004 season Button had developed a close working relationship with David Richards. It was not only professional, but also warm and suffused with mutual respect. Whether they would ever develop the sort of symbiotic partnership that Jackie Stewart enjoyed with the late Ken Tyrrell was another matter, but they had certainly grown very close and were capable of displaying the congenial informality that is usually only the preserve of genuinely good friends.

The author witnessed their lighter side during an informal dinner at the Richards's home near Warwick. We had been casually discussing the merits of the 2003 F1 rule changes for an interview that would form the basis of a feature in *F1 Racing* magazine when the BAR-Honda boss interjected firmly.

'God, don't ask a racing driver about whether or not the rules are good or bad,' he said. 'Ask a representative audience. The problem with this sport so often is that we ask the wrong people just how we should manage it. Instead, what we ought to be doing is the Oxford Street test!'

Jenson cocked his head slightly, looking politely confused. What the hell was the Oxford Street test? Richards replied firmly, 'It involves picking 100 people at random walking down Oxford Street and asking their opinion. And I'll tell you another thing, if you put

Jenson on one side of Oxford Street and Colin McRae on the other, I'll tell you who would be most frequently identified. He [McRae] may have won the World Championship, but it's a measure of F1's status that more people would recognise Jenson.'

Ironically, as far as public recognition was concerned, Jenson's 170mph, brain-rattling accident during the first practice at Monaco in 2003 seemed to have boosted his profile more than any of his on-track achievements. 'The worst thing is that people recognise me a lot more since Monaco,' he said. 'I found it all a bit unbelievable. When I got back to London, I went to see [Professor] Sid Watkins [the FIA medical delegate] on the Tuesday after the accident. That day I saw five people in HMV who came up to me and said "You okay?" It was strange…'

Jenson admitted he had also learned to cope with his fans' intrusive nature. 'It's quite scary when they come to your house,' he said. 'It doesn't happen very often, but it does now and again. And they even come to your motorhome. Somebody came to my motorhome at the Silverstone test when I was having a massage, knocked on the door and because I didn't answer, they just walked in. I said "excuse me, what are you doing?" and she replied "I'm only here for one day", as if that was the answer. But generally everybody is very friendly.'

But how much of a monkey on his back was the lack of a podium finish after four years competing in F1. 'It's very tough, very annoying really,' said Button. 'Every time I have a chance, it's taken away from me through reliability problems. It's not that we've had a particularly unreliable year overall, it's just that when we've been in a crucial situation I haven't been able to finish.'

Yet Richards made no bones about his belief that Jenson had what it takes to win a World Championship, although he knows that raising BAR's game to the necessary level wasn't going to be easy. 'I think in any relationship, if you have mutual respect, and have common goals, you can produce the result,' he said. 'I saw that with Colin [McRae] who seemed an unlikely World Champion at the time; everyone said it wouldn't happen. The same philosophy must work in the F1 business as well. But you've got to have clear goals.

'It's all very well looking up at the top of the podium

John Button and Louise Griffiths, the two most significant people in Jenson's personal life. (Getty Images)

and saying "I'm going to be there", but you've got to work out how you're going to get there and be realistic about how long it's going to take and the steps you're going to take to achieve it. I think that's part of the problem in motor racing. Everybody's looking for short-cuts and there aren't any . . . You can't just throw the dice and hope it will land the right way; it's a long, long process of determination and complete commitment.

'I just feel that Jenson is feeling "Hmm, I've got to step up to the plate now. I'm the one who's going to lead this team" . . . That's going to put a lot of weight

on his shoulders, but I believe he is up to it and that's going to change his approach as well.'

Cynicism, of course, is a journalist's stock in trade, and to say that predictions of the new BAR 006's potential were met with scepticism at the start of 2004 would be something of an understatement. But there was no denying their pre-season confidence. Much was made about the new chassis being stiffer with a lower centre of gravity. It had a smaller fuel tank to reflect the revised qualifying rules, a carbon-composite gearbox maincase and narrow, lightweight gear ratios, which would generate a substantial weight reduction at the rear of the car. But you still had to wonder. Without stating the obvious, everybody else offered wondrous predictions for their new cars' impending form. They couldn't all be right.

The author sustained his cynicism through to qualifying for the first race of 2004, the Australian Grand Prix in Melbourne. Jenson qualified fourth. When Richards told me that Button was not running with a light fuel load, I snorted, 'I'll bet he makes his first refuelling stop before lap ten.' In fact, he came in on lap 11. But it wasn't early compared with his immediate rivals. In the race, he came home a solid sixth. The team was also strengthened when Anthony Davidson was taken on as a full-time third driver. He regularly ran in the Friday free practice sessions, as

Keeping ahead of Fernando Alonso's Renault and the Williams of Juan-Pablo Montoya early in the 2004 Australian Grand Prix. (LAT)

First rostrum. Montoya and Michael Schumacher give Jenson the champagne treatment, Malaysia 2004. (LAT)

pemitted by the changed race weekend format for the new season.

'My start wasn't particularly great,' Button said 'and it was very slippery out there, but I managed to hold on to fourth for some time. Ralf Schumacher's Williams was able to get past me in the pit stop when we had a delay with the refuelling nozzle. Then [Juan Pablo] Montoya got past me out on the circuit. I think we need a little more in the way of race pace, but it's certainly a solid start to the season. We had good reliability, but then so did everybody else.' The Ferrari F2004s of Michael Schumacher and Rubens Barrichello meanwhile finished in commanding 1–2 formation, setting the tone for a season which they would take by storm.

For Button, the key turning point would come at Malaysia's Sepang circuit where he would at last claim his first podium finish with a third place. He qualified sixth and was in the thick of the action from the very start of the chase, getting up to fifth by the end of the second lap after some wheel banging with Jarno Trulli's Renault R24.

Thereafter he never put a wheel wrong. The performance showed that both he and the team had significantly raised their game to challenge for World Championship points in every race. 'It was amazing,' said Button. 'The team has worked so hard. Obviously [it's] not the pinnacle of what we want, but a step in the right direction. I'm ecstatic.'

Having qualified on pole position in conditions that saw the track temperature soar to 53°C, Schumacher capitalised on the slightly cooler conditions that prevailed on race day and pulled away strongly from the start. He had gambled to use the softer of the two Bridgestone tyre compounds, which gave him more grip from the outset.

Coming out of the final corner to take the chequered flag and wave to his pit crew, Schumacher eased off and Montoya closed to within 5 seconds. Yet most observers believed that the German driver's unflustered and composed style throughout the race concealed the fact that he'd held back from asserting his true potential advantage.

Button's third place was not without its problems. The only real moment came when he briefly had to ease off to activate the cockpit control which pumped more oil into the Honda engine from his car's auxiliary tank. His team-mate Takuma Sato had succumbed to an engine failure and the team was taking every precaution to ensure that a similar failure didn't jeopardise Jenson's race.

The most emotional moment of all came about ten minutes after Button emerged from the post-race media conference. As he jogged down the paddock towards the BAR-Honda team garage, he came face to face with his father John and the two men hurled themselves into each other's arms.

Since his boy's graduation into Formula One in 2000, Button senior had been a regular member of the grand prix scene. But he always stood quietly in the background, chatting with other regulars and never seeking to lay claim to any of his son's reflected glory.

'He did it all himself; he deserves it,' said John Button, as Jenson was engulfed by the rest of the BAR squad. They jostled, cheered and reached out to touch the man who'd given them a taste of the respectability and credibility they had been craving since their debut in 1999.

Two years earlier he had been on course for third place at Sepang when his Renault suffered suspension problems in the closing stages and Michael Schumacher's Ferrari, climbing back through the field after an early collision, swept ahead of him on the final lap.

Now the moment had arrived, Jenson could hardly contain himself. 'Melbourne was our first race on Michelins and we gained a lot of information to help us learn how to use them,' he said. 'Initially here we had

too much understeer, and I didn't want to go into the race with an oversteery car. But we sorted that out, which was good.

'At the start, as we passed Mark Webber, I bumped wheels with Jarno [Trulli], which I worried might have damaged the car, but it was all fine. We've worked so hard and it's been a struggle to get on the podium for the first time. It's a fantastic feeling.

'I think the whole team has done a great job over the winter. We have really made a good step forward and that is [includes] everybody in the team. Everybody is really positive, which is great. There is not one person in the team that is negative and we are just making little steps forward every race, getting used to the tyres. We are really happy.'

It was also a hugely satisfying result for David Richards. 'Jenson and the team have worked very hard for this result,' he said, 'and to get his first podium finish in a straight fight with the best in Formula One is real proof of how far we have come.'

The following night, still in Malaysia, Button went out for dinner with David Coulthard, the McLaren driver who was starting out on his final season with the team. 'It was a special evening,' said Jenson. 'I get on with most of the drivers, but we don't hang out, and I

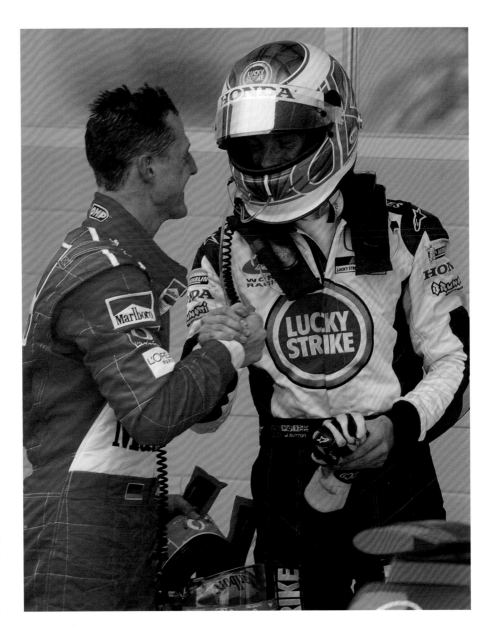

Hugging father John moments after crossing the line to finish third in the Malaysian Grand Prix in Sepang, his first podium finish. (LAT)

Michael Schumacher is the first to congratulate Button after his third place in the 2004 Bahrain Grand Prix. (LAT)

certainly don't share the kind of conversations I have with DC. He said some pretty fantastic words about my race but, at the same time, it is very difficult for him. David has had an amazing career and he's been at McLaren nine years. And now it's not quite clear where he goes next. It's really tough. But he's still quick enough to win – if he gets the right car.'

The third race of the 2004 World Championship was the inaugural Bahrain Grand Prix. It took place on the new Sakhir circuit, another remarkable no-expense-spared constructional *tour de force* situated in the desert scrubland about 20 miles from the Sheikhdom's main city of Manama. Yet again Button's BAR-Honda proved to be the best of the rest as Ferrari's traditional rivals, Williams and McLaren, capitulated in the face of another Maranello grand slam.

When Button joined the two Ferrari drivers on the rostrum, they shared a heady non-alcoholic mix of rosewater and pomegranate juice rather than the usual champagne, in deference to the Arab protocol. The Englishman was third in the World Championship and confident there was more to come from both him and his team. 'This is only our third race with Michelin tyres and working out how they work is not as easy as it seems,' said Button. 'We're gaining experience and hopefully by the next race we can make another step forward.'

In Bahrain, Button had shared a villa at one of the luxury hotels with David Coulthard and his girlfriend Simone, and Mark Webber and his girlfriend Ann Neal. All three drivers get on really well and, despite his own disappointing race, David in particular had become a big fan of the 24-year-old. As they walked together towards the departure gate to catch their British Airways flight back to London on the evening after the race, Coulthard's generous grin as he escorted the similarly beaming Jenson was every bit as dazzling as that on the BAR driver's face.

And so to Imola, and the evocatively titled Autodromo Enzo e Dino Ferrari, the circuit in Maranello's heartland, barely 50 miles from the Italian team's headquarters. Inevitably the 2004 San Marino Grand Prix was a moment for quiet reflection and private grief, marking as it did the tenth anniversary of Ayrton Senna's fatal accident while racing Michael Schumacher's Benetton for the lead.

The weekend saw a raft of tributes to the great man, who died when Jenson was just 14 years old. For many of Formula One's old hands, the events of that painful weekend were still etched in memory. But for guys like Jenson they were part of that tangled and complex tapestry that goes to make up the sport's history. Now it was time for the new guard to make its mark on the record book.

The pace in qualifying looked formidable and, for once, the Ferrari team looked under pressure. The sense of tension was palpable. Ferrari's charismatic president Luca di Montezemolo swung his agile frame on to the pit wall, dressed in open neck shirt and well-cut blue blazer, taking his place alongside the team's forever calm sporting director Jean Todt. This was the customary Maranello theatre, F1's equivalent of a royal

Smiles all round as Jenson and Louise celebrate his pole position at Imola in 2004. (LAT)

visit. And Michael was expected to get the job done for the boss. With some justification.

A few yards further down the pit wall BAR-Honda boss David Richards hauled himself up onto the pit wall next to Geoff Willis. Their faces betrayed the faintest flicker of a smile – smiles of anticipation, perhaps.

The qualifying pace was startlingly quick. The early runners hovered around 1min 21s. Then Spanish star Fernando Alonso dipped down to 1min 20.895sec. Michael's expression tightened slightly. He'd set the pace with a 1min 20.440sec lap in the pre-qualifying session a little earlier, but Alonso was close enough to make him realise that Jenson might be even closer. Under the new qualifying format, Michael would run last having been quickest in pre-qualifying, so he would know the time he had to beat.

Montezemolo punched the air as Barrichello went quickest in the other Ferrari with a lap of 1min 20.451sec. Then it was Jenson's turn. With an economy of effort and meticulous deftness, the BAR-Honda slammed round in 1min 19.753sec. Michael Schumacher looked concerned. But finally he was on his way, tucked deep inside the cockpit of the scarlet Ferrari F2004. He was two-tenths of a second up going into the final sector of the lap. He pushed hard, but at the Variante Alta, a quick right/left chicane four corners from home, he just tried to carry a fraction too much speed into the turn. He slid wide, but gathered it all up in a moment. But it was enough to lose him pole position and he would have to be satisfied with second on 1min 20.011sec. Jenson had taken his first pole.

John Button was standing at the back of the BAR-Honda pit chatting to a group of Jenson's mates who were back in their local pub in Frome. Even over his mobile line, the noise of their cheers and clanking glasses was deafening as Michael completed his

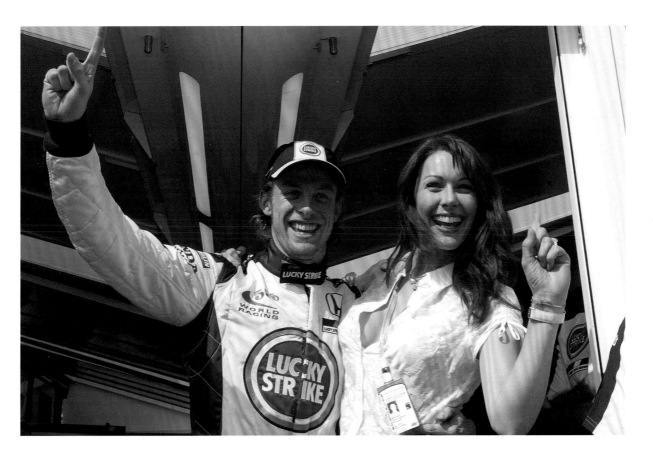

slowing down lap, for once defeated in front of Ferrari's home crowd. Jenson was understandably ecstatic.

'It was a great lap and I enjoyed it very much,' he said, with masterly understatement. 'In pre-qualifying I was a little wide because I had very low grip, but in proper qualifying it seemed to be all there. We set the car up for the race, as everybody does, but we were lacking in qualifying a little bit. But qualifying, of course, is one thing, obviously winning a race is the main goal. I think that's going to be a little bit tougher than today's qualifying. But yeah, I'm looking forward to it. It's the first time in my Formula One career that I've had nobody in front of me at the start, so it's all down to me now.'

David Richards pulled out his now-trademark celebrational cigar and strode down to the back of the BAR transporter where all the mechanics were assembled. 'Well done, guys,' he grinned, shaking them all by the hands. 'Six o'clock in the motorhome. A

glass of champagne. But remember, we're not there yet. We're still aiming for the big one.'

On Saturday there had been another bonus for Jenson as his girfriend Louise Griffiths arrived, fresh off a flight from Australia,with just enough time to give him a good luck kiss before he accelerated out onto the track to take on Schumacher.

After that long Sunday morning – somehow made interminable by the new format, which had eliminated a race day warm-up from the schedule – the moment finally came. Button's BAR took its place on pole position, fussed over with paternal concern by the army of BAR-Honda mechanics. As for Jenson, at last he looked slightly tense. His facial muscles were taut and he looked just a little pale as he pulled on his balaclava and fastened the chin strap on his helmet. One car length behind him Michael Schumacher looked ultra-calm and laid-back, chatting and smiling to friends and cameramen. There was nothing you could tell the six-

Glorious moment: Jenson's BAR-Honda leads the entire field on the opening lap of the 2004 San Marino Grand Prix. (LAT)

times World Champion about high-pressure situations. He'd been through it all.

Button led the pack slowly round the final parade lap. He knew that his Michelin tyres would have more grip than Michael's Bridgestones for the first couple of laps, as the Japanese rubber took longer to come up to temperature. So when the starting lights flickered off, Button accelerated perfectly into an immediate lead as the pack jostled for position into the braking area for the Tamburello chicane.

While Button was making the perfect start from pole, Montoya accelerated his Williams-BMW up from fourth place to within inches of the World Champion's Ferrari as they jinked and weaved their way through the sequence of ess-bends on the outward leg of the circuit.

On the first straight Schumacher weaved across in front of Montoya to prevent him making an overtaking move, then pushed him off the road as he attempted to go around the outside of the Ferrari on the tricky uphill left-hand Tosa hairpin.

'Well, you know Michael had a poor start,' said Montoya. 'He was slow out of the first chicane, you know, the first turns two and three. I went to pass, he closed the door on me and I had to back off. Then he did the same out of the next corner and closed the door.

'So I went for the inside and I'm coming beside him and the next thing I see he's just coming straight at me, hit me and put me up the grass. It's very disappointing to see racing like that, but I'll be surprised if he gets away with it but it's up to the FIA.' He added, 'I actually got in front while we were braking and he says "Oh, he didn't see me there". No chance. You've got to be either blind or stupid not to see me. But you know, it is racing.'

Schumacher eventually escaped without penalty. Meanwhile, Jenson capitalised on the chaos behind him to open up a 2.7sec lead over the Italian car by the end of the opening lap. Perhaps inevitably, by lap four Schumacher had trimmed the advantage to 0.9sec, but Button refused to be ruffled by the pressure. Schumacher admitted he was impressed.

'It was mind blowing what he did in front of me,' he

said. I thought he was driving in the dry and I was driving in the wet. It was then I realised that it was going to be a very busy afternoon.'

Button ducked in to make his first refuelling stop in 9.7sec at the end of lap nine; Schumacher piled on the pressure before making his first stop at the end of lap 11. When the race order settled down again the familiar order had been restored with Schumacher now 6.1sec ahead of the young Englishman.

Thereafter Schumacher held his lead without challenge through his second and third refuelling stop to beat Button by just over nine seconds after easing off

Getting closer! This time Michael has to congratulate him on second place at Imola, 2004. (LAT)

Going for broke. Button's BAR homes in on Trulli's winning Renault. Jenson got close at Monaco, but not quite close enough. (LAT)

on the final lap. Montoya finished a distant third, doubly frustrated by the fact that the new Williams-BMW was clearly unable to challenge the Ferrari F2004 in a straight fight, or the BAR-Honda, for that matter.

Schumacher's praise for Button's performance after the race was certainly satisfying, but equally warming were the positive words from Ferrari technical director Ross Brawn who had watched with fascination as the World Champion strained every sinew to hunt down Jenson in the early stages.

'It was an exciting start to the race because we didn't know quite how much fuel Jenson had on board,' he said. 'He stopped after nine laps, which meant he had 6kg less than Michael, and that was crucial. Michael blitzed his way around the extra two laps he was able to remain out before refuelling. That is why he got ahead and was able to control the pace. But it was, nevertheless, a very impressive performance by Jenson.

'BAR are serious contenders and they did a great job. Jenson had a good race. I am very impressed with him. The signs were there when he was at Williams and his present form just goes to show that when a driver gets the right engineers, the right environment and the team

believe in him, then he raises his game. For him to have taken pole ahead of Schumacher was fantastic and he is learning to work with the team. He is going to become very hot property over the next couple of years.'

Brawn then signalled Ferrari's possible future interest in the young English driver. 'One day Michael is going to stop,' he said, 'and then we will have to look around for a replacement and see who is the best at that stage. Jenson will be on that list.'

David Richards added his perspective to the praise flying around the Imola paddock for the 24 year old. 'This was another encouraging result for Jenson that doesn't surprise me because I have always believed in him,' he said. 'Michael Schumacher would have to make a mistake for Jenson to have a chance of beating him at the moment, but if he's second he has a chance to capitalise should that happen. I still believe he could win a race this year. We will be going to Spain in a fortnight and to other tracks throughout the season and expect to be competitive and do well.'

Honda also saw this achievement as a major boost for their own fortunes after a rough three years back in the Formula One firmament. In particular, Button's

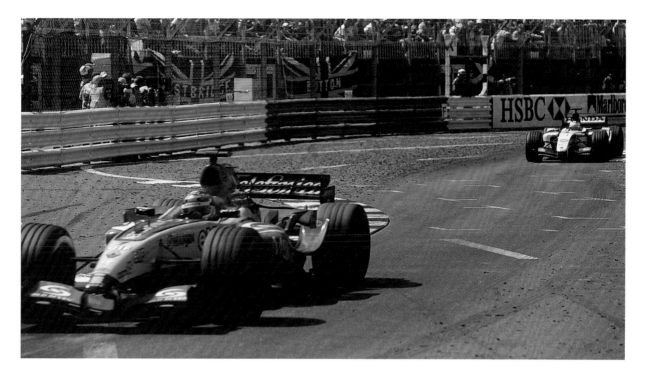

achievement in gaining pole position had something of a wistfully ironic symmetry about it. The last time a Honda engine had been on pole position was at the Canadian GP in 1992. On that occasion, it was Ayrton Senna in his McLaren MP4/7B who had set the pace. The engineer working on the Brazilian's V12 engine was none other than Takeo Kiuchi, who, in 2004, was Honda F1 project leader, or the chief engineer of the Japanese company's F1 programme.

'Jenson's achievement was immense,' said the engineering director of Honda's F1 engine programme, Shuhei Nakamoto. 'To take pole the way he did and then drive so strongly all race really demonstrates his ability and also his obvious confidence in the car. Although we have made a good step this weekend, we have to find the same again to challenge for the top.'

Buoyed by this performance, the team moved on to Barcelona's Circuit de Catalunya for the Spanish Grand Prix. Disappointingly, Button's high hopes evaporated after he made a mistake on his qualifying run and could only line up 14th. Instead it was his team-mate Takuma Sato who kept the BAR-Honda flag flying with an impressive third on the grid behind Michael Schumacher's Ferrari and Juan Pablo Montoya's Williams-BMW.

Come the race, Sato finished a fine fifth, while Jenson climbed back through the field from his lowly grid position to set the second fastest race lap and finish eighth. 'I didn't get a very good start and then I was a little disappointed with the first stint as it just wasn't possible to overtake,' he said. 'I struggled, to be honest. I lost so much time in the high-speed corners because when you're so close to the other cars you lose a lot of downforce.'

The 2004 Monaco Grand Prix kicked off probably the most intense spell of F1 racing in the history of the World Championship. In the following eight weeks there would be no fewer than six races, culminating in Jenson's home event, the British Grand Prix at Silverstone. Ironically at Monaco, it was his former Renault team-mate Jarno Trulli against whom he was pitched in one of the most ferocious battles of his career; the outcome of the race remained in doubt almost to the final corner of the 77th lap.

At the chequered flag Button's BAR-Honda 006 was still 0.497sec adrift in second place after Trulli, who had started from pole position, stoically fought off every challenge the British driver could muster.

Both drivers rose to the challenge of this classic track. They started side-by-side on the front row of the grid and never made a slip throughout a race that claimed several of their more exalted colleagues. Most notably, Michael Schumacher's Ferrari crashed into the barrier in the tunnel after a bizarre incident while running at reduced speed behind the safety car.

Button came to Monaco absolutely determined to make up for the slip at Barcelona. Truth be told, there was nothing to choose between Button's BAR and Trulli's Renault through the sunlit streets of the principality, but it was the Italian who just snatched pole after a scintillating lap on Saturday afternoon.

The safety car was deployed to enable Fernando Alonso's Renault to be dragged to a place of safety after rattling down the barriers to put him out of the race. Then Michael Schumacher's Ferrari, at the head of

Showering Jarno Trulli and Rubens Barrichello on the rostrum after taking second at Monaco, 2004. (LAT)

Wheel to wheel. JB gets close to his pal David Coulthard during the 2004 European Grand Prix at Nürburgring. (LAT)

the slow-moving queue and still to make its second refuelling stop, became embroiled in a collision with Juan Pablo Montoya's Williams FW26, which broke the Ferrari's left-front suspension.

With the World Champion out of the race, it seemed as though Button would be successful in his efforts to hunt down the Renault driver as they headed for the chequered flag. From 5.5sec behind on lap 60, he trimmed Trulli's advantage to 4.1sec on lap 65, 3.5sec on lap 68, 1.6sec on lap 71 and, finally, 0.5sec on lap 74, with just three laps remaining. But he simply couldn't find a way to squeeze by.

'It was a tough and incredibly exciting race for me, and I suspect everybody watching at home too,' said Jenson. 'It felt great crossing the line in second place, but ever so slightly frustrating because I was only a second behind the winner. I didn't get a good start and [Fernando] Alonso was able to get by me. Then the traffic was very bad because of the back markers and I was getting really frustrated, being stuck behind [Cristiano] da Matta for three-and-a-half laps. After I broke free of them, I could really start catching Jarno. We had a great strategy today, but we just couldn't catch him.'

At the Nürburgring a week later, Jenson finished a strong third in the European Grand Prix from fifth on the starting grid. This consolidated his third place in the Drivers' World Championship table with 38 points, two

ahead of Trulli's Renault R24. 'Considering the problem I've had with poor grip throughout the weekend, third place is a great result for me,' said Button. 'Obviously this podium [finish] was slightly more lucky than the other four, but a podium nonetheless. It was a tough race and I had problems with traffic again. I had to get past David [Coulthard] because he was holding me up by two seconds a lap, but fortunately he made a mistake at the last corner and I was able to pass him on the outside. A little bit brave, maybe, but it paid off.'

Across the Atlantic for back-to-back fixtures at Montreal and Indianapolis, Jenson received an unexpected boost to his World Championship ambitions. He was promoted from fourth to third place in the Canadian Grand Prix after both Williams-BMWs and Toyotas were disqualified from the race after they were found to be fitted with illegal front brake cooling ducts.

Ralf Schumacher's subsequent exclusion moved Rubens Barrichello up to second place behind Michael

Jenson watches from the pit wall with David Richards after retiring at Indianapolis, 2004. (LAT)

Schumacher for a Ferrari 1–2 success. Button, meanwhile, moved up to third in his BAR. Juan Pablo Montoya's fourth-placed Williams and the Toyota TF04s of Cristiano da Matta and Olivier Panis, originally eighth and tenth, were also excluded by the FIA race stewards.

Even so, things hadn't looked particularly good during the race itself. 'The race pace just wasn't there,' said Button. 'We came here looking for the win, but when it came to it we weren't quick enough, not even as fast as the Williams, which was a surprise.'

The US Grand Prix at Indianapolis proved to be another disappointment. Button qualified fourth, one place behind his increasingly formidable team-mate Takuma Sato. In the race the team made a strategic error by not bringing them in to refuel when the safety car was deployed to slow the field after Ralf Schumacher's Williams-BMW spun into the wall at 170mph. Ultimately, however, such strategic nuances were irrelevant, as Jenson retired with a gearbox breakage after 26 laps.

Elsewhere in the BAR team, Anthony Davidson had been consistently impressive in his role as the team's third driver. The driver from Hemel Hempstead assiduously worked his way through the Friday free practice session gathering information on every technical parameter, ranging from tyre wear levels to engine performance and fuel consumption. Even

allowing for the fact that the 'Friday testers' were allowed more tyres than the full-time racers, Davidson impressed everybody at Indianapolis by posting second fastest time behind Michael Schumacher.

'At the beginning of the year I was thinking, ah well, it looks like another year's testing for me because there's nothing else on offer,' he said. 'But I thought that perhaps this Friday job might play into my hands and it's turned out to be miles better than I could have ever hoped for. The car has been miles better than we'd ever dreamed of, what with Jenson getting pole position at Imola. We knew it was going to be good, but we're well chuffed.'

'As far as my relationship with Jenson is concerned, it seems to go back as long as I can remember. I can't remember my life without Jenson Button's name being involved, probably since I was eight. We raced together pretty well non-stop in karting from the age of eight until 18, so being in the team together now is almost surreal, bizarre even.

'The strange thing is that, now we're in the same team, we talk about things which happened years ago when we were rivals, things we didn't talk about when we were in different kart teams. It's brilliant being here with him and I hope he feels it's brilliant having me here. We know each other so well we almost know what each other is thinking.'

Jenson with British Deputy PM John Prescott and Sports Minister Richard Caborn at the 2004 British Grand Prix. (LAT)

Returning to Europe, the French Grand Prix at Magny-Cours raised Jenson's hopes again, but after qualifying fourth he wound up fifth, disappointingly frustrated when the BAR's anti-stall mechanism accidentally engaged as he was accelerating out from his final refuelling stop. It slowed him by perhaps a second, maybe a second and a half, but races can be won or lost by such slender margins in today's ferociously competitive F1 environment. On this occasion it made the difference between him taking third, and a place on the rostrum alongside Michael Schumacher and Fernando Alonso, and his disappointing fifth behind Rubens Barrichello and Jarno Trulli, who nipped ahead of him as the BAR momentarily faltered.

Inevitably, the British Grand Prix at Silverstone generated a huge degree of hype and expectancy surrounding Jenson's prospects. As usual at European races, he stayed in his large motorhome tucked away discreetly at the back of the paddock, thereby eliminating the risk of any possible delays getting in and out of the circuit. In his mind it was just another race to be tackled with the same mental discipline, concentration and focus as any other. But deep in his heart, he knew it was something special.

'Obviously, in terms of how I prepare for the race, I don't plan it any differently to the other 17 grands prix,'

he said, 'so going to Silverstone will be the same as going to any other race. However, it is a singularly special experience to actually race in your home country. The British fans always make the whole race weekend seem pretty incredible. In addition, ever since I first raced here as a boy, I have always loved Silverstone. It's very flowing and very quick, one of the original, proper undiluted F1 circuits, so I really enjoy it.'

But it was that tangible emotional support from the fans that set the race apart in Jenson's mind. 'To be honest, in Formula One the fans don't really make any difference to your performance or add any pressure,' he said. 'For footballers, runners or tennis players, they are close to the crowd and so much of their performance is mental. For them, the crowd screaming their support and getting right behind them can inspire them to raise their game, go that extra mile and push on that extra amount.

'In a Formula One car you can't really do that. You can't really push any more than you are already pushing because the crowd is cheering you on, and the car won't go any quicker because they are rooting for you. You obviously notice the crowds and the brilliant support and that's something I'm actually very grateful for, but it doesn't actually affect your speed on the day. You're pushing as hard as you can anyway.

'The parade lap on Sunday morning at Silverstone is when you really notice the fans cheering you on. It's

133

great to see people supporting me and being patriotic with their Union Jack flags and team hats. Also, the noise is incredible. Even over the noise of my Honda V10, and with ear plugs in and a helmet on, I can hear the air horns and the roar of the crowd. It's very special.'

The characteristically capricious British summer weather threatened to turn qualifying at Silverstone on its ear. The format in 2004 meant that every driver did a single flying lap in 'pre-qualifying' and the reversed order of those times would dictate the running order in the battle for grid positions. In ideal conditions, a competitor needed to try ultra-hard in the first session to set quickest time. That would ensure he ran last in the crucial second session, getting out on the track when the grip was traditionally at its best and his prospects of a good grid position very strong.

But at Silverstone there were many teams whose weather forecasters predicted it would rain towards the end of the second session, so spectators were treated to the bizarre sight of some competitors running deliberately slowly in the first session to ensure they would run early in the second before the threatened rain arrived. Michael Schumacher even deliberately spun his Ferrari to waste time. Jenson, fastest in the first session, would go last in the second. Standing in the BAR garage he looked understandably concerned as the skies darkened.

However, David Richards stuck to his guns. 'It won't rain,' he said confidently. The team had a helicopter aloft monitoring conditions. And Richards was correct. Jenson had a dry run, qualifying strongly in third place behind Kimi Raikkönen's impressive new McLaren

Running ahead of Rubens Barrichello's Ferrari in the 2004 British Grand Prix. (LAT)

Jenson sported a new plain red and white helmet design for the 2004 British Grand Prix. (LAT)

Jenson deep in midfield traffic on the opening lap of the 2004 German Grand Prix. (LAT)

MP4/19B and Rubens Barrichello's Ferrari. Yet the race would prove to be a disappointment. The BAR 006 simply lacked the pace to challenge for victory and Jenson had to be content with fourth behind a Schumacher–Barrichello Ferrari 1–3, split by the gallant Raikkönen.

'We came into this race expecting a lot more than we've been able to deliver,' shrugged Jenson. 'Today's race performance was nowhere near our testing performance early in the year. We really struggled with a lack of grip compared to the Ferraris and it was like we were in a different race in terms of the way our car was handling. Our pace showed that we weren't as quick today as we were at the start of the season. Somehow we've managed to drop behind a bit, which is very disappointing, particularly in front of our own crowd. We have a lot of work to do.'

That magical home victory had been denied Button just as it looked as though he would make the key breakthrough. Yet there was still a huge degree of confidence vested in him, both from inside and outside the BAR-Honda team.

'There is an understated quality about Jenson, almost as if he doesn't want to make a lot of noise when he's away from the car and that he would prefer that his performance behind the wheel spoke for his level of achievement alone,' said Damon Hill, who tasted the glory of a home victory when he won the 1994 British Grand Prix at Silverstone.

'I think he could be the sort of driver who thrives on success. He obviously has the speed and the commitment to get the job done. He's in the position, at this stage of his career, when he wants to believe it will happen. But when you've been in Formula One you

Shadowing Alonso's Renault during his climb back to second at Hockenheim, 2004. (LAT)

Another second! Jenson celebrates with a balancing act at Hockenheim. (LAT)

come to appreciate that there are no certainties.

'His big challenge now is to make it happen.'

Two weeks after that rather disappointing run at Silverstone, Jenson found himself battling for second place in the German Grand Prix at Hockenheim, and he drove much of the race one-handed. Many people regarded it as the race of his life, better even than his performance at Imola three months before.

He eventually crossed the finishing line second behind Michael Schumacher's Ferrari F2004, still steadying his helmet with his left hand after the neck strap had worked loose and threatened to strangle him in the 180mph airflow 20 laps short of the finish.

Button grinned with exhaustion as he recounted the experience. 'Towards the end of the race my helmet strap started to work loose and my helmet was lifting down the straights, which was pulling the strap tight against my throat and choking me. I had to drive one-handed for most of the time. I couldn't breathe very well and it was just more worrying than anything else. I was just slightly pulling it down to get more air in.'

Meanwhile, in the pits the BAR engineers were busy examining Button's spare helmet on the assumption that their driver's problem was a loose vizor. They worked out that they could possibly tape it down at the final refuelling stop, but when Jenson fully explained what the problem really was they simply kept their fingers crossed that all would be well. 'This was without

doubt the best race of my Formula One career,' said Button, who had qualified superbly with the third fastest time. But after a ten-place penalty for an engine change during Friday practice had been invoked, he started the contest from a distinctly unpromising 13th in the final grid line up.

'I'm just so thrilled to finish second when I thought the best I could hope for was maybe fifth. The car felt fantastic, the engine was great and the teamwork from the boys was incredible.

'I made a good start but had a terrible first lap and didn't gain anything, but then the team did a fantastic job in the first pit stop. I had a great fight with Fernando [Alonso] who had incredible traction out of turn three where I was losing out to him, then on the straight I could get close to him again. I tried a few times to get past him and nothing seemed to work, but then I finally got him down the inside and held onto it.'

postscript
all change

After his sensational race up through the field from 13th place on the grid to finish second in the German Grand Prix at Hockenheim, Button celebrated with the BAR squad, then vanished on a Mediterranean holiday. Then, just before 17.00 on Thursday, August 5, John Byfield, Button's manager, faxed a letter to David Richards informing the BAR boss that Jenson had signed for Williams in 2005.

Richards's PR offensive immediately went into top gear. Frank Williams, with characteristic discretion, wanted to keep the whole dispute under wraps. But Richards was having no truck with any such censorship. He was absolutely fuming that Button's management was apparently seeking to extricate the 24-year-old from his BAR deal by claiming that the option recently exercised to secure his services in 2005 and beyond was invalid.

'There is absolutely no question, we have a valid contract with Jenson,' said Richards. 'If anything I feel sorry for Jenson at the present moment for being so misled. Both myself and Geoff Willis, our technical director, have been attempting to call him for the last 24 hours, but without any success. This is a quite extraordinary situation.'

Williams, who originally gave Button his F1 chance in 2000, remained confident that their new contract with the British driver was fully valid and he was contractually available to rejoin them next season. 'There has been a long-term relationship between the Williams team and Jenson,' said Frank Williams. 'We have maintained that relationship until the present day, and I am delighted that one of the most talented drivers in Formula 1 has accepted the opportunity to return to the team.'

For his part, Button added, 'I am pleased that I had the option to rejoin the BMW Williams team where my F1 career started. For the meantime the 2004 season

David Richards was distinctly unamused when Jenson burst the Williams bombshell in August 2004. (LAT)

Frank Williams: happy to have the chance with JB second time around. (LAT)

has my full focus and attention. Beyond this, I have every confidence that the massive investment in resources and the depth of talent at Williams and BMW provides the best platform for my future ambitions to be a World Champion.'

Williams added, 'He has been under option to his present team BAR for some time. The option expired recently and Button's management called us to say that the option was no longer valid and would we be interested in his services – and of course I reacted as you might expect me to. I think they [BAR] probably wanted to take up the option but whether they've executed it or not will come out in due course.'

Button's decision was underpinned by his belief that Williams, for all its short-term setbacks, was one of the established blue riband teams with the financial and technical firepower to blast its way back to a position where it could challenge for a World Championship. But Williams knew that BAR would not give up Button without a fight and would insist the whole issue be referred to the FIA Contract Recognition Board. The forum comprises a panel of three international lawyers who meet in Switzerland to adjudicate purely on the conflicting legal aspects of any specific contracts.

'It is our intention to enforce our current contractual position with Jenson,' said Richards. 'My duty is to the 400-strong workforce which has worked tirelessly over the past two seasons to give Jenson the car he has

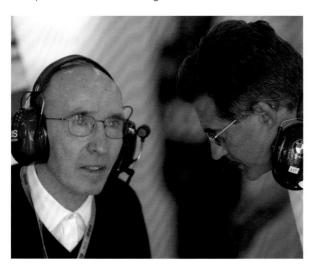

today; and to our partners, whose support and commitment to the team have contributed to the solid structure we now have in place. Unfortunately this is now a matter for the lawyers and I have every confidence that the legal process will confirm that yesterday's announcement has not only been premature but also invalid.'

Williams said he believed that the BAR option was invalid and not exercised properly. 'It all happened a few days before the German Grand Prix,' he said. 'Until then we had assumed that it was out of the question. It was a great surprise. It was an opportunity and we went for it. We have a contract with Jenson and we are of the opinion that BAR lost its opportunity to retain him. One fact is incontestable: Jenson wants and expects to drive for BMW Williams in 2005 and 2006.'

Williams declined to elaborate, but admitted that the BMW Williams team had had 'a form of option on Jenson since the end of 2000'. He added that this had been lodged with the FIA Contract Recognition Board since the end of 2002 and said that this 'was subsidiary to the BAR option'.

For his part, Richards made it clear that Button would race in the Hungarian GP the following weekend as usual. 'We are all a team here at BAR, with one goal and one objective, which is to win races and World Championships,' he said. 'We must treat this matter as a little hiccup, nothing more.'

Frank Williams refused to explain what went wrong with the BAR option on Button, but other sources said that it related to the timing of Honda's confirmation that it was committed to F1 on a long-term basis, one of the key assurances the Button camp was looking for.

Jenson finally met with Richards on Sunday, August 8, to talk over the events of the previous week. In a tense and uneasy exchange, Button explained that he was unshakeable in his determination to drive for Williams in 2005. But Richards made it clear he was not about to be palmed off by claims from either Jenson or his management company, Essentially Sport, that BAR's option on the 24-year-old's services had somehow been incorrectly exercised.

Richards also made it clear that there was no question of standing down Button for any of the remaining races in 2004. 'Jenson has a contract with us to the end of the year. The point of difference between us is whether or not he is committed for next year as well.'

For his part, Button said, 'Given the circumstances, the meeting was constructive. David is now in no doubt of my intention to return to BMW Williams in 2005. My contractual position allows for this. I have also clarified that I am not moving for money, and my motivation is straightforward determination to win a World Championship. Essentially Sport were not permitted to hold private contractual discussions with BAR. I do not feel it was constructive for BAR to leak details of these discussions. Drivers are changing teams up and down the paddock at the moment – an accepted and fundamental element of our sport – and I wish that my return to Williams would have been less acrimonious in light of the contribution I have made to BAR this season.'

An uneasy truce was eventually called between Button and BAR as team personnel began to assemble at the Hungaroring in preparation for the following Sunday's round of the Formula 1 World Championship. The race could conceivably offer Button his best chance yet of posting his maiden Grand Prix victory. The tight, twisty little track was expected to play to the strengths of the agile BAR 006 chassis and its impressively punchy Honda engine.

At the FIA press conference, Button was upbeat about his prospects for the race. 'The atmosphere in the team is okay,' he said. 'It's fine. You know, we're all here to do a job and I am looking forward to it. As soon as we get onto the circuit we are in a position to challenge for a victory, I think.'

'Some of the guys working on the cars may be disappointed with Jenson's decision,' said one team insider, 'but once the action starts out on track all that is pushed to one side. Their naturally competitive instincts kick in and they just want to be the best.'

'The entire team left Germany three weeks ago on an immense high following what was without doubt the best race result in BAR's history,' said Richards. 'The race clearly underlined the fact that we had recovered our advantage over our immediate competitors and we can enjoy a very exciting fight in the remaining six races.'

But the race itself proved to be a disappointment for Button. He qualified fifth and finished fourth. 'I'm a little bit disappointed because we came here expecting better things,' he said. 'I think we might not have put the best condition of tyres on at the first stop, so we lost a lot of time. I had a lot of oversteer which made it very difficult to drive and that's why Jarno [Trulli] was able to get so close to me. Once I made the decision to put a set of conditioned [scrubbed] tyres on then the handling balance was much better.'

With Takuma Sato following Button home in sixth place, BAR could at least console themselves that they had moved to within eight points of Renault in the battle for second place in the constructors' championship, a title clinched for the 14th time by Ferrari thanks to its latest dominant success.

Come the Belgian GP at Spa-Francorchamps, Button's efforts were for nothing as he eventually crashed out in spectacular style at 190mph going into Les Combes, his right rear Michelin blowing out and pitching him straight into Zsolt Baumgartner's Minardi which he was lapping at the time. Thankfully neither was hurt.

By the time he arrived at Monza for the Italian GP, Williams had filed their 2005 contract with the Contract Recognition Board so the process of adjudication could now get seriously underway. In the race it finally looked as although Jenson's long-awaited maiden victory was on the cards. He led commandingly for many laps after both Ferrari drivers found themselves wrong-footed by the initially wet/dry track conditions.

In the end, however, Rubens Barrichello and Michael Schumacher stormed back into contention to finish 1–2 and relegate Jenson to third. 'I just couldn't believe the way they drove past me on the straight without even trying,' he said. 'The pace of those two guys was untouchable. Their performance in the dry was staggering'.

Button's eighth podium finish of the 2004 season at Monza meant that he was all but secure in third place in the Drivers' World Championship, the 'best of the rest' behind the dominant Ferrari drivers. Jenson's on-track performance during 2004 confirmed him as one of Formula 1's hottest properties, and a potential World Champion – his future looks bright…

results

1990
British Cadet karting champion.

1991
British Cadet karting champion winning all 34 races. He also won the British Open Kart Championship.

1992
Won British Open Kart Championship and British Junior TKM titles.

1993
Won British Open Kart Championship for third time.

1994
Fourth in British Junior TKM Kart Championship.

1995
Won Senior ICA Italian Kart Championship. He was the youngest ever runner-up in the Formula A world championship.

1996
Third in both World Cup and American Kart Series.

1997
Won European Supercup A Kart Championship driving for Team GKS Tecno Rotax Bridgestone. Winner of Ayrton Senna Memorial Cup at Suzuka.

1998
Formula Ford
Won TOCA Slick 50 British Championship driving a Mygale for Haywood Racing with nine race wins. Winner Brands Hatch Formula Ford Festival. Runner-up in European FF Championship.

1999
British Formula 3 Championship
Third – three wins (Team Promatecme)

Formula 1
Tests Prost-Peugeot AP02
McLaren-Mercedes MP4/13
Williams-BMW FW21B

2000
Formula 1
Eighth in championship (Williams-BMW) 12 points.

Round	Venue	Grid	Race	Fastest lap
1	Australia	21	DNF (engine)	10th
2	Brazil	9	6th	8th
3	San Marino	18	DNF (engine)	22nd
4	Britain	6	5th	7th
5	Spain	10	17th	4th
6	Europe	11	10th	10th
7	Monaco	14	DNF (oil pressure)	21st
8	Canada	18	11th	16th
9	France	10	8th	11th
10	Austria	18	5th	8th
11	Germany	16	4th	11th
12	Hungary	8	9th	9th
13	Belgium	3	5th	8th
14	Italy	12	DNF (crash)	15th
15	USA	6	DNF (engine)	21st
16	Japan	5	5th	5th
17	Malaysia	16	DNF (engine)	17th

2001
Formula 1
17th in championship (Benetton-Renault) 2 points.

Round	Venue	Grid	Race	Fastest lap
1	Australia	16	14th	15th
2	Malaysia	17	11th	14th
3	Brazil	20	10th	20th
4	San Marino	21	12th	18th
5	Spain	21	15th	18th
6	Austria	21	DNF (engine)	13th
7	Monaco	17	7th	10th
8	Canada	20	DNF (oil leak)	17th
9	Europe	20	13th	14th
10	France	17	16th	16th
11	Britain	18	15th	16th
12	Germany	18	5th	11th
13	Hungary	17	DNF (spin)	14th
14	Belgium	10	DNF (crash)	11th
15	Italy	11	DNF (engine)	18th
16	USA	10	9th	10th
17	Japan	9	7th	9th

2002
Formula 1
7th in championship (Renault) 14 points

Round	Venue	Grid	Race	Fastest lap
1	Australia	11	DNF (crash)	No time
2	Malaysia	8	4th	7th
3	Brazil	7	4th	4th
4	San Marino	9	5th	7th
5	Spain	6	12th	8th
6	Austria	13	7th	7th
7	Monaco	8	DNF (crash)	13th
8	Canada	13	15th	14th
9	Europe	8	5th	4th
10	Britain	12	12th	14th
11	France	7	6th	6th
12	Germany	13	DNF (transmission)	19th
13	Hungary	9	DNF (spin)	16th
14	Belgium	10	DNF (engine)	17th
15	Italy	17	5th	12th
16	USA	14	8th	12th
17	Japan	10	6th	9th

2003
Formula 1
9th equal in championship (BAR-Honda) 17 points

Round	Venue	Grid	Race	Fastest lap
1	Australia	8	10th	7th
2	Malaysia	9	7th	11th
3	Brazil	11	DNF (crash)	13th
4	San Marino	9	8th	8th
5	Spain	5	9th	7th
6	Austria	7	4th	7th
7	Monaco	20	DNS	No time
8	Canada	17	DNF (gearbox)	9th
9	Europe	12	7th	11th
10	France	14	DNF (out of fuel)	10th
11	Britain	20	8th	14th
12	Germany	17	8th	8th
13	Hungary	14	10th	9th
14	Italy	7	DNF (gearbox)	8th
15	USA	11	DNF (hydraulics)	8th
16	Japan	9	4th	6th

2004
Formula 1
BAR-Honda

Round	Venue	Grid	Race	Fastest lap
1	Australia	4	6th	7th
2	Malaysia	6	3rd	3rd
3	Bahrain	6	3rd	5th
4	San Marino	1	2nd	2nd
5	Spain	14	8th	2nd
6	Monaco	2	2nd	3rd
7	Europe	5	3rd	4th
8	Canada	2	3rd	5th
9	USA	4	DNF (gearbox)	5th
10	France	4	5th	5th
11	Britain	3	4th	3rd
12	Germany	13	2nd	2nd
13	Hungary	4	5th	4th
14	Belgium	12	DNF (puncture)	12th
15	Italy	6	3rd	6th

index

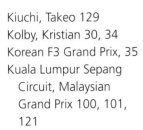